The Ultimate Soup & Stew Cookbook

Dishes, Volume 1

Olivia Bennett

Published by B&H Publishing Group, 2025.

While every precaution has been taken in the preparation of this book, the publisher assumes no responsibility for errors or omissions, or for damages resulting from the use of the information contained herein.

THE ULTIMATE SOUP & STEW COOKBOOK

First edition. February 18, 2025.

Copyright © 2025 Olivia Bennett.

ISBN: 979-8227279217

Written by Olivia Bennett.

Table of Contents

Introduction: The Art of Soups and Stews 1

Chapter 1: Broth-Based Soups 7

Chapter 2: Creamy and Velvety Soups.................................... 13

Chapter 3: Chilled Soups for Warmer Days.................................... 19

Chapter 4: Protein-Packed Soups 25

Chapter 5: Global Flavors in Soups 31

Chapter 6: Traditional Beef Stews 37

Chapter 7: Chicken and Poultry Stews.................................... 44

Chapter 8: Seafood Stews 50

Chapter 9: Vegetarian and Vegan Stews 56

Chapter 10: Rustic and Hearty Stews 62

Chapter 11: Stock and Broth Essentials 68

Chapter 12: Thickening Techniques 74

Chapter 13: One-Pot Wonders 81

Chapter 14: Garnishes and Sides 87

Chapter 15: Cooking for Every Season 92

Bonus Content: Enhancing Your Soup and Stew Game.................................... 98

To the home cooks who find joy in a simmering pot,

To the families and friends gathered around warm, hearty meals,

And to the generations who have passed down recipes, flavors, and traditions—

May every spoonful bring comfort, nourishment, and a taste of love.

This book is for you.

Introduction: The Art of Soups and Stews

Soups and stews hold a timeless place in culinary tradition, celebrated across cultures for their comforting warmth, nourishing properties, and incredible versatility. From a simple bowl of chicken noodle soup on a cold day to a rich, slow-cooked stew that warms the soul, these dishes transcend mere sustenance—they are culinary experiences steeped in history, culture, and emotion.

In this introductory chapter, we explore why soups and stews are the ultimate comfort food, delve into their cultural and historical significance, and provide an overview of the ingredients, tools, and techniques that will guide you through the recipes in this book.

Why Soups and Stews Are the Ultimate Comfort Food

1. Universal Appeal

There's something universally comforting about a bowl of soup or stew. The aroma wafting through the kitchen, the warmth of the broth or sauce, and the harmonious melding of flavors evoke feelings of care, home, and belonging. They are often the dishes we turn to in moments of need—whether we're seeking comfort during illness, sharing a meal with loved ones, or simply warming up on a cold day.

Key Characteristics of Comfort Food in Soups and Stews:

- Warmth: The inherent warmth of soups and stews soothes both body and soul.

- Texture: Creamy soups, hearty broths, and tender chunks in stews offer a variety of textures that appeal to different palates.

- Aroma: The slow cooking process enhances aromas, stimulating the senses even before the first bite.

Example:

A steaming bowl of chicken noodle soup is often synonymous with care and recovery, making it a go-to remedy for colds and flu.

2. Versatility

Soups and stews can be as simple or as complex as you desire. They accommodate a wide range of ingredients, dietary preferences, and cooking methods. Whether you're looking for a light appetizer, a hearty main course, or a vegan-friendly option, there's a soup or stew for every occasion.

Versatile Features:

- Adaptable Ingredients: Use what's in season or what's available in your pantry.

- Dietary Flexibility: Easily modified for vegetarian, vegan, gluten-free, or low-carb diets.

- Scalability: Perfect for single servings, family meals, or large gatherings.

Example:

A basic vegetable soup can transform with the addition of lentils for protein or spices for an international flair, such as cumin for a Middle Eastern touch.

3. Nutritional Value

Beyond their comforting nature, soups and stews are often nutrient-dense. They are excellent vehicles for delivering vitamins, minerals, and proteins, as the slow cooking process preserves nutrients and flavors.

Nutritional Benefits:

- Hydration: Soups contribute to daily fluid intake.

- Balanced Nutrition: A mix of proteins, vegetables, and grains makes soups and stews complete meals.

- Customizable Calories: Light broths for calorie-conscious meals; rich, creamy stews for indulgence.

Example:

A lentil stew enriched with carrots, spinach, and tomatoes provides protein, fiber, and essential vitamins in a single dish.

The Cultural and Historical Significance of Soups and Stews

1. Ancient Roots

The history of soups and stews dates back thousands of years. Archaeological evidence suggests that early humans boiled food as a way to make it more digestible and flavorful. With the advent of fireproof pottery, soups and stews became more refined and central to early diets.

Historical Milestones:

- Prehistoric Cooking: Boiling food in animal skins or clay pots.

- Ancient Civilizations: The Greeks and Romans perfected broths and pottages, while Chinese cuisine introduced medicinal soups.

- Medieval Europe: Stews made with game and grains sustained communities during harsh winters.

Example:

A precursor to modern soups, the Roman *puls* was a porridge-like dish made from grains, legumes, and meat, often considered the ancestor of today's hearty stews.

2. Cultural Diversity

Every culture has its own iconic soups and stews, each reflecting the ingredients, climate, and traditions of its region.

Global Examples:

- France: Bouillabaisse and pot-au-feu showcase the country's culinary sophistication.

- Vietnam: Pho, a fragrant beef noodle soup, embodies the harmony of Vietnamese cuisine.

- Morocco: Tagines, rich with spices and slow-cooked meats, highlight the region's exotic flavors.

- Russia: Borscht, made with beets and sour cream, reflects Eastern Europe's agricultural heritage.

- Mexico: Pozole, a hominy-based stew, celebrates festive occasions and rich flavors.

Example:

The Japanese miso soup, simple yet profound, combines fermented soybean paste, dashi broth, and seasonal ingredients to offer a delicate balance of umami flavors.

3. Soups and Stews in Rituals and Celebrations

Beyond sustenance, soups and stews often hold symbolic value, marking significant life events and celebrations.

Examples of Cultural Significance:

- Weddings: Chicken soup is often served in Jewish weddings as a symbol of prosperity.

- Festivals: Gumbo is a staple in Mardi Gras celebrations, reflecting the cultural melting pot of Louisiana.

- Healing: Many cultures use soups as medicinal remedies, such as Chinese herbal soups or the Jewish *penicillin* chicken soup.

An Overview of the Ingredients, Tools, and Techniques

1. Essential Ingredients

While soups and stews can be made with almost anything, certain ingredients form the backbone of these dishes.

Basic Ingredients:

- Broths and Stocks: Chicken, beef, vegetable, and seafood stocks provide the base.

- Aromatics: Onions, garlic, celery, and carrots are essential for building flavor.

- Proteins: Meat, poultry, seafood, beans, and tofu add substance.

- Vegetables: Seasonal and regional produce enhances both nutrition and taste.

- Herbs and Spices: Fresh and dried herbs, as well as spices like cumin, paprika, and bay leaves, add depth.

Example:

A classic beef stew starts with a base of beef broth, carrots, potatoes, onions, and herbs like thyme and rosemary.

2. Essential Tools

Having the right tools simplifies the cooking process and ensures consistent results.

Key Tools:

- Stockpot: For large batches of soups and stews.
- Dutch Oven: Ideal for slow-cooked stews and braises.
- Immersion Blender: For pureeing creamy soups directly in the pot.
- Slow Cooker or Instant Pot: For hands-free cooking and tender results.
- Ladles and Spoons: For serving and portioning.

Example:

A heavy-bottomed Dutch oven evenly distributes heat, making it perfect for a long-simmered beef bourguignon.

3. Fundamental Techniques

Mastering a few basic techniques ensures your soups and stews turn out perfectly every time.

Key Techniques:

- Sautéing Aromatics: Developing a flavor base by cooking onions, garlic, and spices.
- Deglazing: Adding liquid to a hot pan to release caramelized bits, enhancing depth.
- Simmering: Cooking low and slow for tender ingredients and rich flavors.
- Thickening: Using flour, cornstarch, or pureed vegetables for desired consistency.

Example:

Deglazing a pot with red wine after browning beef enhances the flavor of a hearty stew.

Closing Thoughts

The art of soups and stews is as much about tradition and culture as it is about flavor and nourishment. As you journey through the recipes in this book, you'll not only learn how to create delicious meals but also connect with the rich history and diversity of these timeless dishes. Whether you're seeking comfort on a chilly night, entertaining guests, or exploring international cuisines, the recipes and techniques in this book will empower you to create hearty, satisfying soups and stews for every season. Let's get cooking!

Chapter 1: Broth-Based Soups

Broth-based soups are the foundation of countless recipes across global cuisines. Known for their clear, flavorful base, these soups strike a perfect balance between simplicity and sophistication. Whether you're savoring a light chicken noodle soup, enjoying a hearty bowl of minestrone, or relishing the depth of a perfectly caramelized French onion soup, broth-based soups offer versatility and comfort.

This chapter delves into the fundamentals of making clear broths, explores iconic recipes, and provides tips for enhancing flavor with herbs and aromatics. By mastering these essentials, you'll have the tools to create an array of delicious and nutritious broth-based soups.

The Fundamentals of Making Clear Broths

1. What Is a Broth?

Broth is a clear, flavorful liquid made by simmering ingredients such as meat, bones, vegetables, and seasonings in water. It forms the foundation for many soups and adds depth to countless dishes.

Key Characteristics of Broths:

- Clarity: Unlike stocks, broths are typically strained to achieve a clear appearance.

- Flavor: Balancing the subtle tastes of the ingredients is essential.

- Versatility: Broths can be enjoyed on their own or as a base for more complex soups.

2. Essential Ingredients for Broth

A high-quality broth relies on a few key ingredients:

Proteins:

- Chicken, beef, fish, or pork bones and meat.

- For vegetarian broths, use mushrooms, root vegetables, or seaweed.

Vegetables:

- Common choices include onions, carrots, celery, and garlic.

- Avoid overly starchy or strong-flavored vegetables, such as broccoli or potatoes, which can cloud the broth.
Herbs and Spices:
- Fresh herbs like parsley, thyme, and bay leaves enhance flavor.
- Whole spices like peppercorns, star anise, or cloves add complexity.
Water:
- Use filtered or spring water to prevent off-flavors.

3. The Broth-Making Process

Creating a perfect broth requires attention to detail and patience:
Step 1: Prepare Ingredients
- Rinse meat, bones, and vegetables to remove impurities.
- Roast bones and vegetables (optional) for a richer flavor.
Step 2: Simmer Slowly
- Combine ingredients with cold water in a large pot.
- Heat gently and simmer (never boil) to extract flavors without clouding the broth.
Step 3: Skim Impurities
- Regularly skim off foam and fat that rise to the surface for a clear broth.
Step 4: Strain and Cool
- Strain the broth through a fine-mesh sieve or cheesecloth.
- Cool quickly and store in the refrigerator or freezer.
Pro Tip: Avoid stirring during simmering to prevent cloudiness.

4. Differences Between Broth, Stock, and Consommé

While often used interchangeably, these terms refer to different preparations:
- Broth: A clear liquid made from meat, bones, and vegetables.
- Stock: Richer and more gelatinous, made primarily from bones with longer cooking times.
- Consommé: A clarified broth achieved by simmering with egg whites to remove impurities.

Recipes: Classic Broth-Based Soups

1. Classic Chicken Noodle Soup

Chicken noodle soup is a timeless comfort food, celebrated for its soothing properties and simple yet satisfying flavor.

Ingredients:
- 1 whole chicken (3-4 pounds)
- 2 carrots, diced
- 2 celery stalks, diced
- 1 onion, quartered
- 3 garlic cloves, smashed
- 2 bay leaves
- 8 cups water
- 2 cups egg noodles
- Salt and pepper to taste
- Fresh parsley for garnish

Instructions:

1. Prepare the Broth: Place the chicken, vegetables, garlic, bay leaves, and water in a large pot. Simmer gently for 1.5 to 2 hours, skimming impurities as needed.

2. Strain the Broth: Remove the chicken and strain the broth. Shred the chicken meat and discard the bones.

3. Cook the Noodles: Bring the strained broth to a simmer and cook the egg noodles until tender.

4. Assemble the Soup: Add the shredded chicken back to the pot. Season with salt and pepper, garnish with parsley, and serve hot.

Pro Tip: Enhance flavor by roasting the chicken before making the broth.

2. Hearty Minestrone Soup

Minestrone is a robust Italian soup packed with vegetables, beans, and pasta. It's perfect for using up seasonal produce.

Ingredients:
- 1 tablespoon olive oil
- 1 onion, diced

- 2 carrots, diced
- 2 celery stalks, diced
- 3 garlic cloves, minced
- 1 zucchini, diced
- 1 cup green beans, chopped
- 1 can (14 oz) diced tomatoes
- 6 cups vegetable broth
- 1 can (14 oz) cannellini beans, drained
- 1/2 cup small pasta (e.g., ditalini)
- 1 teaspoon dried oregano
- 1 teaspoon dried basil
- Salt and pepper to taste
- Freshly grated Parmesan cheese for garnish

Instructions:

1. Sauté the Vegetables: Heat olive oil in a large pot and sauté onion, carrots, celery, and garlic until softened.

2. Add Broth and Vegetables: Stir in zucchini, green beans, diced tomatoes, and vegetable broth. Simmer for 20 minutes.

3. Add Pasta and Beans: Add pasta and cannellini beans, cooking until pasta is tender. Season with oregano, basil, salt, and pepper.

4. Serve: Ladle into bowls and top with grated Parmesan.

Pro Tip: Add a Parmesan rind to the broth while simmering for extra richness.

3. Classic French Onion Soup

This rich, caramelized onion soup is a French classic, often served with melted cheese and crusty bread.

Ingredients:
- 4 large onions, thinly sliced
- 2 tablespoons butter
- 1 tablespoon olive oil
- 1 teaspoon sugar
- 4 cups beef broth
- 2 cups chicken broth

- 1/2 cup dry white wine
- 1 baguette, sliced
- 1 cup Gruyère cheese, grated
- Salt and pepper to taste

Instructions:

1. Caramelize the Onions: Heat butter and olive oil in a pot. Add onions and sugar, cooking on low heat for 30-40 minutes until deeply caramelized.

2. Deglaze and Simmer: Add wine to deglaze the pot. Stir in broths and simmer for 20 minutes. Season with salt and pepper.

3. Prepare the Bread: Toast baguette slices until crisp. Top with Gruyère cheese and broil until melted.

4. Serve: Ladle the soup into bowls and top with cheesy bread.

Pro Tip: Use a mix of sweet and yellow onions for balanced flavor.

Tips for Enhancing Flavor with Herbs and Aromatics

1. Use Fresh Herbs: Add fresh parsley, thyme, or dill at the end of cooking for a burst of flavor.

2. Toast Spices: Toasting spices like cumin or coriander before adding them intensifies their aroma.

3. Layer Flavors: Build depth by sautéing aromatics like garlic, onions, and celery before adding liquid.

4. Citrus Zest: Add a touch of lemon or lime zest to brighten the flavor profile.

5. Season Gradually: Taste and adjust seasoning throughout the cooking process.

Closing Thoughts

Broth-based soups are a cornerstone of home cooking, offering endless possibilities for flavor and nourishment. By mastering the fundamentals of broth preparation and incorporating the tips and recipes shared in this chapter, you'll be well-equipped to create comforting, flavorful soups that delight the palate and warm the soul. In the next chapter, we'll explore creamy and velvety soups, diving into techniques that elevate texture and richness. Let's keep cooking!

Chapter 2: Creamy and Velvety Soups

Creamy and velvety soups hold a special place in culinary tradition, offering indulgence and comfort in every spoonful. Their luxurious texture and depth of flavor make them timeless classics, whether served as a starter at a fine dining table or as the centerpiece of a cozy family meal. Achieving that perfect velvety texture requires a combination of technique, the right ingredients, and an understanding of how to balance flavors, particularly the interplay of richness and acidity.

In this chapter, we'll explore the techniques for creating creamy soups using both dairy and non-dairy alternatives, share three beloved recipes—cream of mushroom, potato leek soup, and roasted tomato bisque—and discuss how to balance the richness of these soups with acidity to create harmonious dishes.

Techniques for Achieving the Perfect Texture

1. Understanding Creamy Soup Texture

The hallmark of a great creamy soup is its smooth, velvety consistency. This texture is achieved by blending ingredients and incorporating rich, creamy elements that add body and depth. It's essential to strike a balance—too thin, and the soup lacks substance; too thick, and it feels heavy.

Key Components of Creamy Soups:

- Base Ingredients: Vegetables, proteins, or legumes provide the foundation.

- Thickening Agents: Dairy (cream, milk, butter), non-dairy substitutes, or pureed vegetables create a creamy texture.

- Blending: Proper blending ensures smoothness.

- Seasoning and Flavor Balance: Herbs, spices, and acids enhance and refine the flavor.

2. Blending Techniques for Smoothness

1. Immersion Blender:

- A handheld immersion blender allows you to puree the soup directly in the pot.

- Best for quick blending and minimal cleanup.

2. Stand Blender:

- Produces a finer texture, making it ideal for soups like bisques.

- Blend in batches to avoid overfilling and prevent accidents.

3. Food Processor:

- Useful for coarser purees but may not achieve the same smoothness as a blender.

Pro Tip: Always let the soup cool slightly before blending to avoid pressure buildup in closed appliances.

3. Incorporating Dairy and Non-Dairy Alternatives

Dairy Options:

- Heavy Cream: Adds richness and a silky texture.

- Milk: A lighter alternative for less indulgent soups.

- Butter: Enhances flavor and gives a glossy finish.

- Cheese: Parmesan, Gruyère, or cream cheese can be blended in for added depth.

Non-Dairy Options:

- Coconut Milk or Cream: Adds a subtle sweetness, ideal for global-inspired soups.

- Cashew Cream: Soaked and blended cashews mimic the richness of dairy.

- Almond Milk: A lighter alternative with a mild nutty flavor.

- Silken Tofu: Blends smoothly for a protein-packed, creamy consistency.

4. Thickening Techniques

Vegetable Purees:

- Pureeing starchy vegetables like potatoes, squash, or cauliflower naturally thickens soups.

Roux:

- A mixture of butter and flour cooked together, added to the soup for a classic thickening agent.

Slurry:

- A mix of cornstarch or arrowroot and water, stirred in for a gluten-free thickening option.

Rice or Oats:

- Simmering and blending cooked rice or oats adds creaminess and body.

5. Balancing Flavors

Rich, creamy soups can sometimes feel overly heavy without the right balance of flavors. Incorporating acidity and contrasting elements ensures a more refined taste.

Ways to Balance Richness:

- Acidity: A splash of lemon juice, vinegar, or wine brightens flavors.
- Herbs: Fresh parsley, thyme, or dill adds freshness.
- Spices: Ground pepper, paprika, or nutmeg enhances depth.
- Garnishes: Croutons, crispy bacon, or a drizzle of olive oil adds texture and contrast.

Recipes: Creamy and Velvety Soups

1. Cream of Mushroom Soup

Cream of mushroom soup is a classic, offering earthy flavors and a velvety texture that's both indulgent and comforting.

Ingredients:

- 2 tablespoons butter
- 1 tablespoon olive oil
- 1 onion, finely chopped
- 3 garlic cloves, minced
- 1 pound cremini or button mushrooms, sliced
- 2 tablespoons all-purpose flour
- 4 cups chicken or vegetable broth
- 1 cup heavy cream
- 1 teaspoon thyme leaves
- Salt and pepper to taste
- Fresh parsley for garnish

Instructions:

1. Sauté the Aromatics: Heat butter and olive oil in a pot. Sauté the onion and garlic until softened.

2. Cook the Mushrooms: Add the mushrooms and thyme, cooking until they release their liquid and begin to brown.

3. Make the Roux: Sprinkle flour over the mushrooms, stirring to coat. Cook for 2 minutes to eliminate the raw flour taste.

4. Add Broth: Gradually pour in the broth while stirring. Simmer for 15 minutes.

5. Blend: Use an immersion blender to puree the soup until smooth.

6. Finish with Cream: Stir in the heavy cream and season with salt and pepper. Garnish with parsley and serve hot.

Pro Tip: For an extra layer of flavor, add a splash of dry sherry or white wine before adding the broth.

2. Potato Leek Soup

Potato leek soup is a French-inspired dish known for its creamy texture and delicate flavor.

Ingredients:
- 2 tablespoons butter
- 3 large leeks, white and light green parts sliced
- 4 medium potatoes, peeled and diced
- 4 cups chicken or vegetable broth
- 1 cup milk or cream
- 1/2 teaspoon nutmeg
- Salt and pepper to taste
- Fresh chives for garnish

Instructions:

1. Prepare the Leeks: Wash leeks thoroughly to remove dirt and sand.

2. Sauté the Leeks: Melt butter in a pot and sauté leeks until softened but not browned.

3. Cook the Potatoes: Add diced potatoes and broth. Simmer until potatoes are tender, about 20 minutes.

4. Blend: Use an immersion blender or stand blender to puree the soup until smooth.

5. Finish with Cream: Stir in milk or cream, nutmeg, and season with salt and pepper. Garnish with chives and serve.

Pro Tip: For a vegan version, substitute cream with coconut milk or almond milk.

3. Roasted Tomato Bisque

This roasted tomato bisque combines the sweetness of roasted tomatoes with the richness of cream for a perfectly balanced soup.

Ingredients:
- 2 pounds ripe tomatoes, halved
- 1 onion, quartered
- 4 garlic cloves
- 2 tablespoons olive oil
- 2 cups vegetable broth
- 1 cup heavy cream or coconut milk
- 1 teaspoon dried basil
- 1 teaspoon sugar
- Salt and pepper to taste
- Fresh basil leaves for garnish

Instructions:

1. Roast the Vegetables: Preheat the oven to 400°F (200°C). Arrange tomatoes, onion, and garlic on a baking sheet. Drizzle with olive oil and roast for 25-30 minutes.

2. Simmer: Transfer roasted vegetables to a pot. Add broth, dried basil, and sugar. Simmer for 15 minutes.

3. Blend: Use an immersion blender or stand blender to puree the soup until smooth.

4. Finish with Cream: Stir in heavy cream or coconut milk. Season with salt and pepper. Garnish with fresh basil before serving.

Pro Tip: Roasting the tomatoes enhances their natural sweetness and depth of flavor.

How to Balance Richness with Acidity

1. The Role of Acidity in Creamy Soups

Acidity cuts through the richness of cream-based soups, creating a more balanced and enjoyable dish. It enhances flavors, prevents heaviness, and adds brightness.

Acidic Ingredients to Use:
- Lemon or lime juice
- Vinegars (balsamic, white wine, or apple cider)
- Dry white wine or sherry
- Tomatoes or tomato paste

2. Garnishes for Contrast

Adding a garnish not only elevates the presentation but also introduces contrasting textures and flavors.

Examples of Garnishes:
- A drizzle of balsamic glaze for tanginess.
- Fresh herbs like dill, chives, or parsley for brightness.
- Crispy croutons or fried shallots for texture.

Closing Thoughts

Creamy and velvety soups are more than just indulgent—they are versatile canvases for creativity, texture, and flavor. Whether you're crafting a classic cream of mushroom soup, a comforting potato leek soup, or an elegant roasted tomato bisque, the techniques and tips in this chapter will help you achieve restaurant-quality results at home. In the next chapter, we'll explore chilled soups for warmer days, offering refreshing recipes perfect for spring and summer. Let's continue mastering the art of soups!

Chapter 3: Chilled Soups for Warmer Days

Chilled soups are a refreshing answer to hot summer days and balmy evenings. Unlike their warm counterparts, these soups are designed to invigorate with light, crisp flavors and cool textures. They draw from seasonal ingredients like fresh vegetables, fruits, and herbs, creating dishes that are as visually appealing as they are delicious. From the bright, bold notes of gazpacho to the creamy elegance of vichyssoise, chilled soups are versatile and ideal for both casual gatherings and sophisticated presentations.

This chapter will guide you through the art of creating refreshing cold soups, featuring classic recipes such as gazpacho, vichyssoise, and chilled cucumber dill soup. We'll also share tips on serving these soups with style to elevate any dining experience.

The Art of Creating Refreshing Cold Soups

1. What Makes a Great Chilled Soup?

A great chilled soup is defined by its balance of flavor, texture, and temperature. While warm soups rely on heat to blend flavors, chilled soups emphasize the natural freshness of ingredients. Achieving the right balance requires careful attention to seasoning, consistency, and presentation.

Key Characteristics of Chilled Soups:

- Freshness: Ingredients like ripe vegetables, fresh herbs, and citrus create a bright, clean taste.

- Texture: Ranges from silky smooth (vichyssoise) to chunky (gazpacho).

- Temperature: Proper chilling enhances the flavors and provides a refreshing sensation.

2. Techniques for Perfect Chilled Soups

1. Blend for Smoothness or Texture:
   - Use a high-speed blender for silky smooth soups like vichyssoise.

- Opt for a food processor or hand chopping for chunkier soups like gazpacho.

2. Season Generously:

- Chilled soups often need more seasoning than warm soups, as cold temperatures dull flavors slightly.

3. Chill Thoroughly:

- Allow soups to chill in the refrigerator for at least two hours before serving. This not only enhances flavor but also ensures the right temperature.

4. Strain for Refinement:

- For ultra-smooth soups, strain the mixture through a fine sieve.

5. Use High-Quality Ingredients:

- With fewer ingredients, the quality of produce becomes more critical. Use the freshest and ripest available.

3. Balancing Flavors

Cold soups benefit from a balance of acidity, sweetness, and spice to keep flavors vibrant.

- Acidity: Lemon juice, lime juice, or vinegar adds brightness.
- Sweetness: A touch of honey or ripe fruits balances acidity.
- Spice: Chili, black pepper, or garlic creates depth.

Example:

Adding a splash of sherry vinegar to gazpacho enhances its tanginess and complements the sweetness of ripe tomatoes.

Recipes: Chilled Soups for Every Occasion

1. Gazpacho: A Spanish Classic

Gazpacho is a traditional Spanish soup that captures the essence of summer. Made with ripe tomatoes, crisp cucumbers, and bell peppers, it's a perfect combination of freshness and flavor.

Ingredients:

- 6 ripe tomatoes, chopped
- 1 cucumber, peeled and diced
- 1 red bell pepper, chopped

- 1 small red onion, chopped
- 2 garlic cloves, minced
- 3 tablespoons olive oil
- 2 tablespoons red wine vinegar
- 2 cups tomato juice
- Salt and black pepper to taste
- Fresh basil or parsley for garnish

Instructions:

1. Blend the Vegetables: Combine tomatoes, cucumber, bell pepper, onion, and garlic in a blender. Blend until smooth.

2. Add Liquids: Add olive oil, red wine vinegar, and tomato juice. Blend again until well combined.

3. Season and Chill: Season with salt and pepper. Refrigerate for at least two hours before serving.

4. Serve: Garnish with fresh basil or parsley and a drizzle of olive oil. Serve cold.

Pro Tip: For a more textured gazpacho, reserve some diced vegetables to stir in before serving.

2. Vichyssoise: French Elegance

Vichyssoise is a creamy, chilled leek and potato soup of French origin. Its velvety texture and subtle flavor make it a sophisticated addition to any meal.

Ingredients:
- 4 leeks, white and light green parts only, sliced
- 2 medium potatoes, peeled and diced
- 2 tablespoons butter
- 4 cups chicken or vegetable stock
- 1 cup heavy cream
- Salt and white pepper to taste
- Chives for garnish

Instructions:

1. Sauté the Leeks: Melt butter in a pot. Sauté leeks until softened but not browned.

2. Cook the Potatoes: Add potatoes and stock. Simmer until potatoes are tender, about 20 minutes.

3. Blend and Chill: Blend the soup until smooth. Stir in cream and season with salt and white pepper. Chill for at least two hours.

4. Serve: Garnish with chopped chives and serve cold.

Pro Tip: For a lighter version, substitute cream with unsweetened almond milk.

3. Chilled Cucumber Dill Soup

This refreshing soup combines cool cucumbers with the brightness of dill and yogurt for a light and tangy summer dish.

Ingredients:

- 3 cucumbers, peeled and diced
- 2 cups plain Greek yogurt
- 1 cup vegetable broth
- 2 tablespoons fresh dill, chopped
- 2 garlic cloves, minced
- 1 tablespoon lemon juice
- Salt and black pepper to taste
- Thin cucumber slices and dill sprigs for garnish

Instructions:

1. Blend the Ingredients: Combine cucumbers, yogurt, vegetable broth, dill, garlic, and lemon juice in a blender. Blend until smooth.

2. Season and Chill: Season with salt and pepper. Refrigerate for at least two hours.

3. Serve: Garnish with cucumber slices and dill sprigs. Serve chilled.

Pro Tip: Add a small avocado to the blender for an extra creamy texture.

Presentation Tips for Serving Chilled Soups Elegantly

1. Use Beautiful Serving Ware

Chilled soups deserve a presentation that highlights their vibrant colors and textures.

- Glass Bowls or Cups: Showcase the soup's color and garnishes.
- Chilled Bowls: Pre-chill serving bowls in the refrigerator to maintain the soup's temperature.
- Shot Glasses: For appetizers, serve chilled soups in shot glasses for a stylish touch.

2. Garnish Thoughtfully

A well-chosen garnish enhances both flavor and visual appeal.

- Herbs: Use fresh herbs like basil, dill, or cilantro for a pop of color.
- Croutons: Add crunch with homemade croutons or toasted seeds.
- Drizzles: A swirl of olive oil, yogurt, or balsamic reduction adds elegance.
Example:
Top gazpacho with diced vegetables, a drizzle of olive oil, and a sprinkle of smoked paprika for a rustic yet refined presentation.

3. Pair with Complementary Sides

Elevate the dining experience by serving chilled soups with complementary sides:

- Crusty Bread: A warm baguette or sourdough complements creamy soups like vichyssoise.
- Light Salads: A mixed green salad pairs beautifully with gazpacho.
- Cheese Plates: Offer a selection of cheeses to balance the lightness of chilled soups.

4. Add Creative Elements

For a contemporary twist, consider these presentation ideas:

- Layered Soups: Create layers of different soups in clear glasses for a stunning visual effect.
- Edible Flowers: Add a touch of elegance with edible flowers like pansies or nasturtiums.

- Serve in Edible Bowls: Hollow out bell peppers, cucumbers, or small melons as natural serving vessels.

Closing Thoughts

Chilled soups are a testament to the versatility of soup as a dish, offering refreshing flavors and elegant presentation options that celebrate the best of summer's bounty. By mastering the techniques and recipes in this chapter, you'll be able to create stunning soups that impress guests and bring a touch of sophistication to your warm-weather meals. In the next chapter, we'll dive into protein-packed soups, exploring hearty recipes that satisfy hunger while delivering balanced nutrition. Let's keep cooking!

Chapter 4: Protein-Packed Soups

Protein-packed soups are the ultimate fusion of nourishment and flavor, offering meals that satisfy hunger and fuel the body. These soups go beyond mere sustenance by incorporating meats, legumes, and plant-based proteins like tofu to create hearty, balanced dishes. Whether you're looking for a comforting bowl of beef barley soup, a nutrient-dense lentil soup, or a savory miso soup with tofu, protein-packed soups provide versatility and nutritional benefits for every palate.

This chapter will explore how to incorporate various proteins into soups, present three classic recipes, and guide you on pairing proteins with the right herbs and spices to enhance their flavor.

The Role of Protein in Soups

1. Why Protein Matters

Protein is a vital macronutrient that supports muscle growth, repair, and overall health. Including protein in soups transforms them into complete meals, making them both satisfying and nutritionally balanced.

Benefits of Protein in Soups:

- Satiety: Keeps you full for longer periods.
- Versatility: Works well with a variety of ingredients and flavor profiles.
- Nutrition: Provides essential amino acids and nutrients like iron, zinc, and B vitamins.

2. Common Protein Options

Soups are adaptable to a range of protein sources, from hearty meats to plant-based alternatives.

Meats:
- Chicken, beef, pork, lamb, and seafood offer rich flavors and textures.
- Perfect for slow-cooked soups like stews or broths.

Legumes:

- Lentils, chickpeas, and beans are excellent plant-based protein options.
- They also add fiber and make soups heartier.
Tofu and Plant-Based Proteins:
- Tofu, tempeh, and seitan absorb flavors beautifully in broths and spices.
- Ideal for vegetarian and vegan soups.
Eggs:
- Used in soups like egg drop or ramen, eggs provide quick and easy protein.

3. Balancing Protein with Other Ingredients

Protein-packed soups require the right balance of vegetables, grains, and seasonings to achieve a harmonious flavor and texture.

Tips for Balance:

- Pair proteins with starchy vegetables or grains like potatoes, barley, or rice for a complete meal.

- Use fresh herbs and spices to enhance natural flavors without overpowering the protein.

- Incorporate a variety of textures by combining soft proteins (tofu) with crunchy vegetables.

Recipes: Protein-Packed Soups

1. Beef Barley Soup

Beef barley soup is a classic, hearty dish that combines tender beef, nutty barley, and a medley of vegetables in a rich broth.

Ingredients:

- 1 pound beef stew meat, cubed
- 2 tablespoons olive oil
- 1 onion, diced
- 3 carrots, sliced
- 2 celery stalks, sliced
- 3 garlic cloves, minced
- 1/2 cup pearl barley
- 6 cups beef broth
- 1 bay leaf

- 1 teaspoon thyme
- Salt and pepper to taste
- Fresh parsley for garnish

Instructions:

1. Brown the Beef: Heat olive oil in a large pot. Brown the beef cubes, then remove and set aside.

2. Sauté Vegetables: Add onion, carrots, celery, and garlic to the pot. Sauté until softened.

3. Add Barley and Broth: Return beef to the pot and stir in barley, broth, bay leaf, and thyme.

4. Simmer: Cover and simmer for 1.5 to 2 hours, or until beef is tender and barley is cooked.

5. Season and Serve: Remove the bay leaf, season with salt and pepper, and garnish with parsley.

Pro Tip: Use a mix of beef broth and water to control the soup's saltiness.

2. Lentil Soup

Lentil soup is a nutrient-rich, plant-based option packed with protein, fiber, and flavor. It's a versatile recipe that can be customized with your favorite vegetables and spices.

Ingredients:

- 1 tablespoon olive oil
- 1 onion, diced
- 2 carrots, diced
- 2 celery stalks, diced
- 3 garlic cloves, minced
- 1 cup dried lentils (green or brown), rinsed
- 6 cups vegetable broth
- 1 teaspoon cumin
- 1 teaspoon paprika
- 1/2 teaspoon turmeric
- 1 can (14 oz) diced tomatoes
- Salt and pepper to taste
- Fresh parsley or cilantro for garnish

Instructions:

1. Sauté Aromatics: Heat olive oil in a pot. Sauté onion, carrots, celery, and garlic until softened.

2. Add Lentils and Spices: Stir in lentils, cumin, paprika, and turmeric. Cook for 1 minute to toast the spices.

3. Simmer: Add broth and tomatoes. Simmer for 30-40 minutes, or until lentils are tender.

4. Season and Serve: Season with salt and pepper. Garnish with fresh parsley or cilantro before serving.

Pro Tip: For a creamier texture, blend half the soup and mix it back into the pot.

3. Miso Soup with Tofu

Miso soup is a traditional Japanese dish that features tofu as the primary protein source. Light yet flavorful, it's perfect as a starter or a light meal.

Ingredients:
- 4 cups dashi broth (or vegetable broth)
- 3 tablespoons white miso paste
- 1 block firm tofu, cubed
- 1/2 cup sliced shiitake mushrooms
- 1/2 cup seaweed (wakame), soaked and drained
- 2 green onions, sliced

Instructions:

1. Prepare the Broth: Heat dashi broth in a pot over medium heat. Do not let it boil.

2. Add Tofu and Mushrooms: Stir in tofu cubes, mushrooms, and wakame. Simmer for 5 minutes.

3. Incorporate Miso: Remove a small amount of broth and whisk it with miso paste to dissolve. Stir the miso mixture back into the pot.

4. Serve: Garnish with green onions and serve warm.

Pro Tip: Add a splash of soy sauce or a few drops of sesame oil for extra flavor.

Pairing Proteins with the Right Herbs and Spices

1. Pairing Meats

Meats require bold flavors that enhance their richness without overpowering them.

- Beef: Thyme, rosemary, bay leaf, black pepper.
- Chicken: Parsley, tarragon, sage, lemon zest.
- Pork: Fennel seed, garlic, paprika, oregano.

Example:

Beef barley soup benefits from earthy thyme and bay leaf, which complement the richness of the beef.

2. Pairing Legumes

Legumes absorb spices well, making them ideal for global-inspired soups.

- Lentils: Cumin, coriander, turmeric, smoked paprika.
- Chickpeas: Garlic, rosemary, chili flakes, lemon juice.
- Beans: Bay leaf, thyme, onion powder, cayenne.

Example:

Lentil soup gains depth from cumin and paprika, while turmeric adds a warm, golden hue.

3. Pairing Tofu and Plant-Based Proteins

Tofu and plant-based proteins are like blank canvases, absorbing the flavors of the broth and seasonings.

- Tofu: Soy sauce, ginger, garlic, miso.
- Tempeh: Curry powder, chili paste, coconut milk.
- Seitan: Sage, thyme, black pepper, mustard.

Example:

Miso soup with tofu shines with the addition of umami-rich miso paste and green onions for a fresh finish.

Enhancing Protein-Packed Soups

1. Adding Textural Contrast

Protein-packed soups benefit from contrasting textures, such as crunchy toppings or creamy garnishes.
- Crunchy Additions: Croutons, toasted seeds, fried onions.
- Creamy Toppings: Yogurt, sour cream, or coconut milk drizzle.

2. Serving Suggestions

Protein-packed soups can be standalone meals or paired with complementary sides:
- Bread: Serve with crusty sourdough, cornbread, or naan.
- Salads: Pair with a light green salad or coleslaw.
- Grains: Add cooked rice, quinoa, or farro for extra substance.

Closing Thoughts

Protein-packed soups are a testament to how nourishing and flavorful a single bowl can be. By mastering the techniques and recipes in this chapter, you'll be able to create hearty, satisfying soups that cater to a variety of tastes and dietary needs. Whether it's the rich depth of beef barley soup, the nutrient-dense warmth of lentil soup, or the delicate umami of miso soup with tofu, these recipes will leave you and your guests feeling both satisfied and inspired. In the next chapter, we'll explore global flavors in soups, traveling through iconic recipes from around the world. Let's continue this culinary journey!

Chapter 5: Global Flavors in Soups

Soups are universal comfort food, but they are as diverse as the cultures that create them. Across the globe, soups reflect local ingredients, traditions, and culinary practices, making them a window into the soul of a culture. Whether it's the fragrant broth of Vietnamese pho, the vibrant colors of Eastern European borscht, or the spicy, coconut-infused laksa from Malaysia, each soup tells a unique story.

In this chapter, we'll explore the flavors of three iconic soups from different parts of the world, delving into their cultural significance, key ingredients, and preparation methods. We'll also highlight the spices and herbs that make these soups distinct, providing a deeper understanding of how global cuisines use seasonings to create depth and character.

Exploring Soups from Different Cuisines

1. The Role of Soups in Global Cuisines

Every culture has its own take on soup, influenced by geography, history, and local ingredients. While some soups are light and refreshing, others are hearty and robust, serving as meals in themselves. Soups are often designed to:
- Celebrate Seasonal Ingredients: Using fresh produce at its peak.
- Sustain Communities: Providing nourishment and warmth during colder months.
- Heal and Rejuvenate: Many soups have medicinal properties, using herbs and spices for their health benefits.
- Bring People Together: Shared bowls of soup often symbolize unity and hospitality.

2. Common Elements in Global Soups

While ingredients vary widely, many global soups share common elements:
- Broths: Chicken, beef, fish, or vegetable stocks serve as the base.
- Proteins: Meat, seafood, legumes, or tofu provide substance.
- Vegetables: Seasonal produce adds texture and nutrition.

- Spices and Herbs: These define the soup's cultural identity.

3. Highlighting Three Iconic Soups

Let's explore three beloved soups: pho from Vietnam, borscht from Eastern Europe, and laksa from Malaysia. Each of these soups embodies the flavors and traditions of its region, showcasing the versatility of this universal dish.

Recipes: Iconic Soups from Around the World

1. Pho (Vietnamese)

Pho is a traditional Vietnamese noodle soup characterized by its fragrant broth and simple yet deeply satisfying ingredients. A dish that originated as street food, pho has become a global favorite for its delicate balance of flavors.

Ingredients (Serves 4):

- 8 cups beef broth (or chicken for lighter pho)
- 1 pound beef bones or chicken carcass (optional for homemade broth)
- 1 onion, halved
- 4-inch piece of ginger, sliced
- 4 star anise pods
- 2 cinnamon sticks
- 2 cloves
- 1 tablespoon fish sauce
- 8 ounces rice noodles
- 8 ounces thinly sliced beef (sirloin or brisket)
- Fresh herbs (cilantro, Thai basil)
- Bean sprouts, lime wedges, and sliced chili for garnish

Instructions:

1. Prepare the Broth: In a large pot, combine broth, beef bones (if using), onion, ginger, star anise, cinnamon, and cloves. Simmer for 2-3 hours, skimming impurities as needed.

2. Season the Broth: Strain the broth and season with fish sauce. Adjust salt to taste.

3. Cook the Noodles: Prepare rice noodles according to package instructions. Drain and set aside.

4. Assemble the Bowls: Divide noodles into bowls, top with raw sliced beef, and ladle hot broth over to cook the meat.

5. Garnish and Serve: Add fresh herbs, bean sprouts, lime wedges, and sliced chili.

Pro Tip: For an authentic experience, serve with hoisin sauce and sriracha on the side.

Understanding Vietnamese Spices and Herbs:

- Star Anise and Cinnamon: Create the signature warmth and aroma.

- Fish Sauce: Adds umami and depth.

- Thai Basil and Cilantro: Provide a fresh, herbal finish.

2. Borscht (Eastern European)

Borscht is a vibrant beet soup popular in Eastern Europe, particularly in Ukraine and Russia. Known for its striking red color and sweet-sour flavor, borscht can be served hot or cold, often accompanied by a dollop of sour cream.

Ingredients (Serves 4):

- 3 medium beets, peeled and grated

- 1 onion, diced

- 2 carrots, diced

- 2 potatoes, peeled and cubed

- 4 cups beef or vegetable broth

- 1/2 head of cabbage, shredded

- 1 can (14 oz) diced tomatoes

- 2 tablespoons vinegar or lemon juice

- 2 tablespoons sugar

- 1 bay leaf

- Salt and pepper to taste

- Sour cream and fresh dill for garnish

Instructions:

1. Cook the Vegetables: In a pot, sauté onion, carrots, and beets until softened.

2. Simmer the Soup: Add broth, potatoes, cabbage, tomatoes, bay leaf, vinegar, and sugar. Simmer for 20-30 minutes, until all vegetables are tender.

3. Season and Serve: Remove bay leaf, season with salt and pepper, and ladle into bowls. Garnish with sour cream and dill.

Pro Tip: Roasting the beets before adding them enhances their sweetness.

Understanding Eastern European Spices and Herbs:

- Bay Leaf: Adds depth and earthiness.
- Dill: A classic herb that brightens the soup.
- Vinegar or Lemon Juice: Balances sweetness with tang.

3. Laksa (Malaysian)

Laksa is a spicy, coconut-based noodle soup that is a cornerstone of Malaysian cuisine. Combining the creaminess of coconut milk with the heat of chili and the tang of tamarind, laksa is a bold, flavorful dish.

Ingredients (Serves 4):

- 2 tablespoons laksa paste (store-bought or homemade)
- 1 tablespoon vegetable oil
- 1 can (14 oz) coconut milk
- 4 cups chicken or vegetable broth
- 8 ounces rice noodles
- 1 cup cooked chicken or shrimp
- 1 cup bean sprouts
- Fresh cilantro and mint for garnish
- Lime wedges for serving

Instructions:

1. Cook the Laksa Paste: Heat oil in a pot and sauté laksa paste until fragrant.

2. Prepare the Broth: Stir in coconut milk and broth. Simmer for 10 minutes.

3. Cook the Noodles: Prepare rice noodles according to package instructions.

4. Assemble the Bowls: Divide noodles into bowls, add cooked chicken or shrimp, and pour hot broth over.

5. Garnish and Serve: Top with bean sprouts, cilantro, mint, and lime wedges.

Pro Tip: Adjust the spice level by adding more or less laksa paste.

Understanding Malaysian Spices and Herbs:

- Laksa Paste: A blend of chili, lemongrass, turmeric, and shrimp paste creates the soup's signature flavor.

- Coconut Milk: Adds creaminess and balances the heat.

- Lime and Tamarind: Provide acidity to brighten the soup.

Understanding Spices and Herbs Unique to Each Culture

1. Vietnamese Spices and Herbs (Pho):

- Cinnamon and Star Anise: Add warmth and a sweet-spicy aroma.

- Thai Basil and Cilantro: Enhance the freshness of the broth.

- Ginger: Provides a subtle heat that complements the soup's lightness.

2. Eastern European Spices and Herbs (Borscht):

- Dill: A staple herb that cuts through the sweetness of beets.

- Bay Leaf: Adds a savory undertone.

- Vinegar or Lemon Juice: Balances the soup's earthy flavors.

3. Malaysian Spices and Herbs (Laksa):

- Chili and Lemongrass: Infuse the soup with heat and citrusy brightness.

- Turmeric: Adds an earthy flavor and vibrant color.

- Coconut Milk: Balances the spiciness with creamy richness.

Enhancing Global Soups

1. Pairing with Sides

- Pho: Serve with spring rolls or banh mi for a complete Vietnamese meal.

- Borscht: Pair with rye bread or garlic rolls.

- Laksa: Offer crispy prawn crackers or roti on the side.

2. Presentation Tips

- Use vibrant garnishes to highlight the soup's colors.

- Serve in traditional bowls for an authentic touch.

- Include condiments like chili oil, hoisin sauce, or sour cream for customization.

Closing Thoughts

Global soups like pho, borscht, and laksa showcase the incredible diversity and depth of flavor that soups can offer. By exploring these iconic recipes, you not only expand your culinary repertoire but also connect with the rich traditions of their respective cultures. In the next chapter, we'll delve into rustic and hearty stews that celebrate slow-cooked comfort and robust flavors. Let's continue this journey of culinary discovery!

Chapter 6: Traditional Beef Stews

Few dishes can match the warmth and satisfaction of a well-made beef stew. Rooted in tradition and perfected over centuries, these slow-cooked masterpieces transform tough cuts of beef into tender, flavorful morsels swimming in a rich, savory broth. Traditional beef stews not only celebrate the art of slow cooking but also showcase the deep, layered flavors created through careful use of ingredients like wine, beer, and aromatic herbs.

This chapter will guide you through the fundamentals of slow-cooking beef, highlight three classic recipes—beef stew, boeuf bourguignon, and Irish stew—and explore how to use wine, beer, and broths to elevate the flavors of your stew.

The Basics of Slow-Cooking Tough Cuts of Beef

1. Why Tough Cuts Are Ideal for Stews

Tough cuts of beef, such as chuck, brisket, and shank, are rich in connective tissue and marbling. When cooked slowly, the collagen in these cuts breaks down into gelatin, creating a silky, flavorful texture that defines great stews.

Benefits of Using Tough Cuts:

- Flavorful: The higher fat content and connective tissue add richness.

- Economical: Tough cuts are often more affordable than premium cuts.

- Perfect for Slow Cooking: Long, gentle cooking transforms these cuts into tender, melt-in-your-mouth bites.

Common Cuts for Stews:

- Chuck Roast: Known for its balance of fat and flavor.

- Brisket: Ideal for stews that require a longer cooking time.

- Shank: Adds depth and body to the broth.

- Oxtail: Offers a gelatinous texture and intense beefy flavor.

2. Preparing Beef for Stews

Proper preparation ensures that the beef retains its flavor and texture throughout the cooking process.

Steps to Prepare Beef:

1. Trim Excess Fat: Remove any large, thick pieces of fat to prevent a greasy stew.

2. Cut into Uniform Pieces: Cut beef into 1.5-2 inch cubes for even cooking.

3. Season Generously: Season with salt and pepper before browning.

4. Sear for Flavor: Brown the beef in a hot pan with oil to develop a deep, caramelized crust. This step adds complexity to the stew.

Pro Tip: Do not overcrowd the pan when searing, as this can steam the beef instead of browning it.

3. The Importance of Low and Slow Cooking

Slow cooking allows the flavors to meld and the beef to tenderize over time. Whether you're using a Dutch oven, slow cooker, or pressure cooker, maintaining a low temperature is key.

Optimal Cooking Times:

- Stovetop or Oven: 2.5 to 3 hours at a low simmer or 325°F in the oven.

- Slow Cooker: 6 to 8 hours on low heat.

- Pressure Cooker: 35 to 45 minutes under high pressure.

Recipes: Traditional Beef Stews

1. Classic Beef Stew

This traditional beef stew combines tender chunks of beef with hearty vegetables in a rich, flavorful broth. It's a perfect comfort food for chilly days.

Ingredients:

- 2 pounds beef chuck, cut into 2-inch cubes

- 2 tablespoons olive oil

- 1 onion, diced

- 2 garlic cloves, minced
- 4 carrots, sliced
- 3 celery stalks, sliced
- 4 medium potatoes, peeled and cubed
- 3 tablespoons all-purpose flour
- 4 cups beef broth
- 1 cup dry red wine (optional)
- 2 tablespoons tomato paste
- 1 teaspoon thyme
- 1 bay leaf
- Salt and pepper to taste
- Fresh parsley for garnish

Instructions:

1. Brown the Beef: Heat olive oil in a large Dutch oven. Sear beef in batches until browned. Remove and set aside.

2. Sauté Vegetables: Add onion, garlic, carrots, and celery to the pot. Cook until softened.

3. Deglaze and Build the Broth: Stir in flour and cook for 1 minute. Add beef broth, wine, tomato paste, thyme, and bay leaf, scraping up browned bits from the bottom of the pot.

4. Simmer: Return beef to the pot and add potatoes. Cover and simmer on low heat for 2.5 hours, stirring occasionally.

5. Season and Serve: Remove the bay leaf, season with salt and pepper, and garnish with parsley before serving.

Pro Tip: For a richer flavor, let the stew rest overnight in the refrigerator and reheat before serving.

2. Boeuf Bourguignon (French Beef Stew)

This classic French stew, made famous by Julia Child, uses red wine as a key ingredient, resulting in a deeply flavorful and elegant dish.

Ingredients:
- 2 pounds beef chuck, cut into 2-inch cubes
- 6 slices bacon, diced
- 1 onion, diced

- 2 carrots, sliced
- 2 garlic cloves, minced
- 2 tablespoons tomato paste
- 2 cups dry red wine
- 2 cups beef broth
- 1 bay leaf
- 1 teaspoon thyme
- 1/2 pound mushrooms, quartered
- 1 tablespoon butter
- Salt and pepper to taste

Instructions:

1. Brown the Bacon: In a Dutch oven, cook bacon until crisp. Remove and set aside.

2. Sear the Beef: Sear beef cubes in the rendered bacon fat until browned. Remove and set aside.

3. Cook Vegetables: Add onion, carrots, and garlic to the pot. Cook until softened.

4. Build the Broth: Stir in tomato paste, then deglaze with wine. Add beef broth, bay leaf, thyme, and the reserved bacon and beef.

5. Simmer: Cover and simmer for 2.5 hours.

6. Cook Mushrooms: Sauté mushrooms in butter until browned. Stir into the stew during the last 30 minutes of cooking.

7. Season and Serve: Remove the bay leaf, season to taste, and serve with crusty bread or over mashed potatoes.

Pro Tip: Use a Burgundy or Pinot Noir wine for authentic flavor.

3. Irish Stew

Irish stew is a rustic dish traditionally made with lamb or beef, root vegetables, and simple seasonings. Its hearty, comforting flavors make it a favorite in Irish households.

Ingredients:

- 2 pounds beef chuck or lamb shoulder, cut into chunks
- 2 tablespoons olive oil
- 1 onion, sliced

- 2 garlic cloves, minced
- 4 medium potatoes, peeled and sliced
- 2 carrots, sliced
- 4 cups beef or lamb broth
- 1 cup Guinness beer (optional)
- 1 teaspoon rosemary
- 1 teaspoon thyme
- Salt and pepper to taste
- Fresh parsley for garnish

Instructions:

1. Brown the Meat: Heat olive oil in a pot. Sear beef or lamb until browned. Remove and set aside.

2. Layer Vegetables: In the same pot, layer onion, garlic, potatoes, and carrots. Add the seared meat on top.

3. Build the Broth: Pour in broth and beer. Add rosemary and thyme. Bring to a simmer.

4. Cook: Cover and simmer for 2.5 hours, or until meat is tender and vegetables are cooked.

5. Season and Serve: Adjust seasoning with salt and pepper. Garnish with parsley before serving.

Pro Tip: For a thicker stew, mash some of the potatoes into the broth before serving.

Using Wine, Beer, and Broths to Elevate Flavors

1. Wine in Stews

Wine enhances the depth and complexity of stews by adding acidity and richness.

- Red Wine: Ideal for beef stews like boeuf bourguignon, adding robust flavors.

- White Wine: Complements lighter stews with subtle acidity.

Pro Tip: Always use a wine you enjoy drinking for the best results.

2. Beer in Stews

Beer, particularly darker varieties, adds a malty sweetness and depth to stews.

- Stout (e.g., Guinness): Perfect for Irish stew, offering a robust, slightly bitter profile.

- Amber Ale: Adds a toasty, caramelized flavor.

Pro Tip: Balance the bitterness of beer with a touch of sugar or tomato paste.

3. Broths as a Base

Broths form the foundation of a good stew. Choose broths that complement your ingredients.

- Beef Broth: Adds richness and enhances meaty flavors.

- Chicken Broth: Works well for lighter stews.

- Vegetable Broth: Suitable for vegetarian options.

Pro Tip: Simmering homemade broth with bones and aromatics yields superior flavor.

Enhancing Stews with Herbs and Spices

1. Common Herbs for Beef Stews

- Thyme and Rosemary: Add earthy notes.

- Bay Leaf: Enhances depth.

- Parsley: Brightens the final dish.

2. Spices for Warmth

- Black Pepper and Paprika: Add subtle heat.

- Nutmeg or Allspice: Complement hearty flavors.

Closing Thoughts

Traditional beef stews embody the art of slow cooking, transforming humble ingredients into meals of extraordinary depth and flavor. By mastering the techniques and recipes in this chapter, you'll be able to create classic stews that honor their rich culinary heritage while delighting modern palates. In the next chapter, we'll explore chicken and poultry stews, diving into recipes and techniques that showcase their versatility and flavor. Let's keep cooking!

Chapter 7: Chicken and Poultry Stews

Chicken and poultry stews are beloved worldwide for their versatility, flavor, and ability to comfort on any occasion. These dishes, which range from rustic one-pot meals to elegantly spiced creations, transform simple ingredients into deeply satisfying meals. Whether it's the Southern charm of chicken and dumplings, the French sophistication of coq au vin, or the exotic allure of Moroccan chicken tagine, poultry stews offer endless possibilities for both home cooks and seasoned chefs.

This chapter explores how to prepare tender, flavorful poultry for stews, provides detailed recipes for three classic dishes, and delves into the art of balancing light and hearty ingredients for perfectly harmonious stews.

How to Prepare Stews with Tender, Flavorful Poultry

1. Choosing the Right Poultry

The type of poultry you select will significantly influence the flavor and texture of your stew. While chicken is the most common choice, turkey, duck, and even quail can also be used, depending on the dish.

Best Cuts for Stews:

- Bone-In, Skin-On Chicken Thighs: These provide rich flavor and retain moisture during cooking.

- Drumsticks: Perfect for hearty stews and easy to handle.

- Whole Chicken, Cut into Pieces: Offers a mix of textures and flavors from different cuts.

- Breasts: Suitable for lighter stews but prone to drying out if overcooked.

Pro Tip: Dark meat (thighs and drumsticks) is more forgiving in stews due to its higher fat content and natural tenderness.

2. Preparing Poultry for Stews

Proper preparation ensures the poultry remains tender and flavorful throughout the cooking process.

Steps to Prepare Poultry:

1. Trimming: Remove excess fat and skin if desired.

2. Seasoning: Season generously with salt and pepper before cooking to enhance flavor.

3. Searing: Brown the chicken pieces in a hot pan with oil before adding them to the stew. This step locks in juices and adds depth to the dish.

4. Removing Skin (Optional): While skin adds flavor, it can make the stew greasy. Consider removing it after searing.

Pro Tip: If using whole chicken pieces, shred the meat after cooking and return it to the stew for easier serving.

3. Techniques for Tender Poultry

Cooking poultry in a stew requires care to avoid overcooking or drying out the meat.

Key Techniques:

- Low and Slow Cooking: Simmer chicken gently to allow the flavors to meld without toughening the meat.

- Layered Cooking: Add delicate ingredients like breasts or vegetables later in the cooking process to prevent overcooking.

- Using Acidic Marinades: Ingredients like lemon juice, yogurt, or vinegar tenderize the meat and add brightness to the stew.

Recipes: Classic Chicken and Poultry Stews

1. Chicken and Dumplings

A Southern classic, chicken and dumplings is a hearty dish featuring tender chicken, creamy broth, and fluffy dumplings.

Ingredients (Serves 4):

- 1 whole chicken (3-4 pounds), cut into pieces
- 2 tablespoons olive oil
- 1 onion, diced
- 2 carrots, sliced
- 2 celery stalks, sliced
- 3 garlic cloves, minced
- 6 cups chicken broth

- 1 cup heavy cream
- 1 teaspoon thyme
- Salt and pepper to taste
- Fresh parsley for garnish
For the Dumplings:
- 1 1/2 cups all-purpose flour
- 2 teaspoons baking powder
- 1/2 teaspoon salt
- 2/3 cup milk
- 3 tablespoons butter, melted
Instructions:

1. Brown the Chicken: Heat olive oil in a large pot. Sear chicken pieces until golden brown. Remove and set aside.

2. Sauté Vegetables: Add onion, carrots, celery, and garlic to the pot. Cook until softened.

3. Build the Broth: Return chicken to the pot, add chicken broth, and bring to a simmer. Add thyme, cover, and cook for 1 hour.

4. Make the Dumplings: In a bowl, combine flour, baking powder, and salt. Stir in milk and melted butter until just combined.

5. Add Cream and Dumplings: Stir cream into the stew. Drop spoonfuls of dumpling dough onto the surface of the stew. Cover and cook for 15-20 minutes, or until dumplings are puffed and cooked through.

6. Season and Serve: Remove chicken pieces, shred the meat, and return it to the stew. Season with salt and pepper, garnish with parsley, and serve.

Pro Tip: For extra flavor, add a bay leaf to the broth while simmering.

2. Coq au Vin

A French classic, coq au vin features chicken braised in red wine with mushrooms, onions, and bacon, creating a rich and elegant dish.

Ingredients (Serves 4):
- 4 bone-in chicken thighs
- 4 drumsticks
- 6 slices bacon, diced
- 1 onion, diced

- 2 garlic cloves, minced
- 2 cups red wine (Burgundy or Pinot Noir)
- 2 cups chicken broth
- 2 tablespoons tomato paste
- 1 bay leaf
- 1 teaspoon thyme
- 1/2 pound mushrooms, sliced
- 2 tablespoons butter
- Salt and pepper to taste

Instructions:

1. Brown the Bacon and Chicken: In a Dutch oven, cook bacon until crisp. Remove and set aside. Brown chicken pieces in the bacon fat, then remove and set aside.

2. Sauté Vegetables: Add onion, garlic, and mushrooms to the pot. Cook until softened.

3. Deglaze and Build the Broth: Stir in tomato paste, then deglaze with wine. Add chicken broth, bay leaf, and thyme. Return chicken and bacon to the pot.

4. Simmer: Cover and cook on low heat for 1.5 hours, or until chicken is tender.

5. Finish and Serve: Remove bay leaf, season with salt and pepper, and serve with crusty bread or mashed potatoes.

Pro Tip: For a lighter version, substitute white wine for red.

3. Moroccan Chicken Tagine

This spiced Moroccan stew is a feast for the senses, combining tender chicken, preserved lemons, and olives in a flavorful, aromatic sauce.

Ingredients (Serves 4):
- 4 chicken thighs
- 4 drumsticks
- 2 tablespoons olive oil
- 1 onion, sliced
- 3 garlic cloves, minced
- 1 teaspoon ground ginger

- 1 teaspoon ground cinnamon
- 1 teaspoon paprika
- 1/2 teaspoon turmeric
- 2 cups chicken broth
- 1 preserved lemon, quartered
- 1 cup green olives
- Fresh cilantro for garnish

Instructions:

1. Brown the Chicken: Heat olive oil in a tagine or heavy-bottomed pot. Sear chicken pieces until golden. Remove and set aside.

2. Cook the Onions and Spices: Add onion, garlic, ginger, cinnamon, paprika, and turmeric to the pot. Cook until fragrant.

3. Build the Sauce: Return chicken to the pot, add chicken broth, preserved lemon, and olives. Bring to a simmer.

4. Simmer: Cover and cook on low heat for 1.5 hours, or until chicken is tender.

5. Finish and Serve: Garnish with fresh cilantro and serve with couscous or flatbread.

Pro Tip: If you can't find preserved lemons, use fresh lemon slices and a pinch of salt.

Balancing Light and Hearty Ingredients

1. Creating Harmony in Stews

Balancing light and hearty ingredients is key to crafting a well-rounded stew. While poultry provides a rich protein base, vegetables, grains, and aromatics lighten the dish and add complexity.

Tips for Balance:

- Combine robust flavors (bacon, wine, preserved lemons) with mild ingredients (carrots, potatoes, rice).

- Add acidic elements like vinegar or citrus to cut through richness.

- Use fresh herbs to brighten heavy stews.

2. Layering Flavors

Layering flavors throughout the cooking process enhances depth and complexity.

- Aromatics: Sauté garlic, onions, and spices early to build a flavor foundation.

- Broth Enhancements: Use wine, tomato paste, or spices to enrich the liquid.

- Finishing Touches: Stir in fresh herbs or cream at the end for brightness and texture.

3. Pairing with Sides

Complement poultry stews with sides that enhance their flavors:

- Chicken and Dumplings: Serve with a side of green beans or a light salad.

- Coq au Vin: Pair with mashed potatoes, crusty bread, or buttered noodles.

- Moroccan Chicken Tagine: Accompany with couscous, flatbread, or a minty yogurt dip.

Closing Thoughts

Chicken and poultry stews highlight the versatility and richness of these proteins, offering something for every palate. From the comforting simplicity of chicken and dumplings to the exotic flavors of Moroccan tagine, these recipes and techniques will help you master the art of creating tender, flavorful stews. In the next chapter, we'll explore seafood stews, diving into dishes that showcase the ocean's bounty with depth and elegance. Let's keep cooking!

Chapter 8: Seafood Stews

Seafood stews offer a delightful combination of delicate flavors, rich broths, and the bounty of the sea. These stews often carry the essence of coastal traditions, making them deeply rooted in regional cuisines around the world. Whether you're savoring the hearty Italian-American cioppino, the French sophistication of bouillabaisse, or the bold, tropical flavors of coconut curry shrimp stew, seafood stews promise a dining experience that is both comforting and elegant.

This chapter will guide you through the techniques for cooking seafood stews without overcooking delicate proteins, provide detailed recipes for three iconic seafood stews, and offer tips for sourcing fresh seafood and using high-quality frozen alternatives.

Cooking Seafood Stews Without Overcooking Delicate Proteins

1. The Challenge of Cooking Seafood

Seafood proteins, such as fish, shellfish, and mollusks, are naturally delicate. Overcooking can lead to rubbery textures and diminished flavors. Achieving the perfect seafood stew requires precise timing and gentle cooking methods.

Why Seafood Overcooks Easily:

- Low Collagen Content: Unlike meat, seafood lacks connective tissues, so it cooks quickly.

- Delicate Texture: The fine structure of seafood proteins breaks down under high heat.

2. Techniques for Perfectly Cooked Seafood

1. Stagger Cooking Times:

- Different types of seafood cook at different rates. For instance, shrimp may cook in 2-3 minutes, while firm fish like cod or halibut may take 5-7 minutes. Add seafood to the stew in stages based on their cooking times.

2. Use Gentle Heat:

- Simmer, don't boil. High heat can toughen seafood. A gentle simmer ensures even cooking and preserves texture.

3. Cook in Broth:

- Cooking seafood directly in the stew's broth infuses it with flavor while preventing it from drying out.

4. Remove Seafood When Done:

- To avoid overcooking, remove seafood from the stew as soon as it's cooked through. Return it to the pot just before serving to warm it up.

3. Selecting the Right Seafood for Stews

Firm-Fleshed Fish:

- Cod, halibut, sea bass, and salmon hold their shape well in stews.

Shellfish:

- Shrimp, scallops, and lobster add sweetness and texture.

Mollusks:

- Clams and mussels open naturally when cooked and enrich the broth with their briny essence.

Crustaceans:

- Crab adds richness and pairs well with spiced broths.

Recipes: Iconic Seafood Stews

1. Cioppino

Cioppino is a hearty Italian-American seafood stew that originated in San Francisco. This tomato-based stew combines a variety of seafood with wine and aromatic herbs, making it a comforting yet elegant dish.

Ingredients (Serves 4):

- 2 tablespoons olive oil

- 1 onion, diced

- 3 garlic cloves, minced

- 1 red bell pepper, diced

- 1 can (14 oz) diced tomatoes

- 1 cup dry white wine

- 4 cups fish stock or clam juice
- 1 teaspoon dried oregano
- 1 teaspoon red pepper flakes
- 1 pound firm white fish (e.g., cod or halibut), cut into chunks
- 1/2 pound shrimp, peeled and deveined
- 1/2 pound scallops
- 12 mussels or clams, scrubbed
- Fresh parsley for garnish
- Crusty bread for serving

Instructions:

1. Sauté Aromatics: Heat olive oil in a large pot. Sauté onion, garlic, and bell pepper until softened.

2. Build the Broth: Stir in tomatoes, wine, fish stock, oregano, and red pepper flakes. Simmer for 15 minutes.

3. Add Seafood: Add fish and simmer for 5 minutes. Add shrimp, scallops, and mussels or clams. Cover and cook until shellfish open and shrimp turn pink (about 3-4 minutes). Discard any unopened shellfish.

4. Season and Serve: Season with salt and pepper. Garnish with parsley and serve with crusty bread.

Pro Tip: Enhance the broth with a splash of Pernod (an anise-flavored liqueur) for added depth.

2. Bouillabaisse

Bouillabaisse is a traditional Provençal seafood stew that blends fish, shellfish, and aromatic herbs in a saffron-infused broth. It's a dish that exemplifies the elegance of French cuisine.

Ingredients (Serves 4):
- 2 tablespoons olive oil
- 1 leek, thinly sliced
- 2 garlic cloves, minced
- 1 fennel bulb, thinly sliced
- 1 can (14 oz) diced tomatoes
- 1/2 cup dry white wine
- 4 cups fish stock

- 1/2 teaspoon saffron threads
- 1 pound firm white fish (e.g., monkfish or snapper), cut into chunks
- 1/2 pound shrimp, peeled and deveined
- 12 mussels or clams, scrubbed
- 1/4 teaspoon cayenne pepper
- Fresh thyme and bay leaf
- Rouille sauce (for serving)
- Crusty bread

Instructions:

1. Sauté Vegetables: Heat olive oil in a pot. Sauté leek, garlic, and fennel until softened.

2. Build the Broth: Add tomatoes, wine, fish stock, saffron, thyme, bay leaf, and cayenne. Simmer for 20 minutes.

3. Add Seafood: Add fish and shrimp to the pot and cook for 5 minutes. Add mussels or clams and cook until they open. Discard any unopened shellfish.

4. Serve: Serve the stew with rouille sauce and crusty bread.

Pro Tip: For an authentic touch, prepare homemade rouille by blending garlic, red pepper, and olive oil into a smooth paste.

3. Coconut Curry Shrimp Stew

This tropical-inspired stew combines the creaminess of coconut milk with the bold flavors of curry and lime, creating a dish that is both comforting and vibrant.

Ingredients (Serves 4):

- 2 tablespoons vegetable oil
- 1 onion, diced
- 2 garlic cloves, minced
- 1 tablespoon ginger, grated
- 2 tablespoons red curry paste
- 1 can (14 oz) coconut milk
- 2 cups chicken or vegetable broth
- 1 pound shrimp, peeled and deveined
- 1 cup diced sweet potatoes

- 1 cup spinach leaves
- 1 lime, juiced
- Fresh cilantro for garnish
- Steamed jasmine rice for serving

Instructions:

1. Sauté Aromatics: Heat oil in a pot. Sauté onion, garlic, and ginger until fragrant. Stir in curry paste.

2. Build the Broth: Add coconut milk, broth, and sweet potatoes. Simmer until sweet potatoes are tender.

3. Add Shrimp and Spinach: Add shrimp and cook until pink (about 3 minutes). Stir in spinach until wilted.

4. Season and Serve: Add lime juice and season with salt. Garnish with cilantro and serve over rice.

Pro Tip: Add a splash of fish sauce for an extra layer of umami.

Tips for Sourcing Fresh Seafood

1. Selecting Fresh Seafood

Fresh seafood is key to a flavorful stew. Look for the following signs of freshness:

- Fish: Clear eyes, firm flesh, and a mild ocean scent.
- Shellfish: Tightly closed shells or shells that close when tapped.
- Shrimp: Firm texture and a translucent appearance.

2. Using Frozen Seafood

High-quality frozen seafood can be a convenient alternative to fresh. Look for seafood that is:

- Individually Quick Frozen (IQF): This method preserves texture and flavor.
- Wild-Caught: Often higher in quality and flavor.
- Free of Additives: Avoid products with excessive preservatives or sodium tripolyphosphate.

3. Storing and Thawing Seafood

Proper storage and thawing ensure seafood retains its quality:

- Storage: Keep fresh seafood refrigerated and use within 1-2 days. Store frozen seafood in a deep freezer.
- Thawing: Thaw frozen seafood overnight in the refrigerator or under cold running water. Avoid thawing at room temperature.

Enhancing Seafood Stews

1. Layering Flavors

Use aromatics, herbs, and spices to build a complex flavor profile:

- Aromatics: Onions, garlic, ginger, and fennel.
- Herbs: Fresh thyme, parsley, and cilantro.
- Spices: Saffron, curry paste, and red pepper flakes.

2. Pairing with Sides

Complement seafood stews with sides that enhance their flavors:

- Cioppino: Serve with garlic bread or a mixed green salad.
- Bouillabaisse: Pair with rouille-topped bread and a glass of white wine.
- Coconut Curry Shrimp Stew: Offer steamed jasmine rice or naan bread.

Closing Thoughts

Seafood stews capture the essence of coastal cuisines, celebrating the natural flavors of the ocean with each bite. By mastering the techniques and recipes in this chapter, you'll be able to create dishes that impress and satisfy, whether you're hosting a dinner party or enjoying a quiet night in. In the next chapter, we'll explore vegetarian and vegan stews, showcasing the creativity and depth that plant-based cooking can bring to your table. Let's continue cooking!

Chapter 9: Vegetarian and Vegan Stews

Vegetarian and vegan stews showcase the versatility and depth of plant-based cooking, proving that meat isn't necessary to create hearty, satisfying meals. These stews rely on the natural flavors of vegetables, legumes, grains, and spices, with techniques designed to build complexity and richness. From the rustic charm of ratatouille to the bold flavors of vegetable curry stew and the comforting warmth of black bean chili, these dishes highlight the potential of plant-based cuisine.

In this chapter, we'll explore how to create depth of flavor without meat, share detailed recipes for three classic vegetarian and vegan stews, and discuss how to incorporate plant-based proteins and dairy substitutes for rich, nourishing meals.

Creating Depth of Flavor Without Meat

1. The Challenges of Flavor in Plant-Based Stews

Traditional stews often rely on meat for flavor, particularly through fats, browning, and umami compounds. Vegetarian and vegan stews require alternative methods to achieve similar complexity and satisfaction. The goal is to create a stew that feels complete and balanced, with layers of taste and texture.

2. Techniques for Building Flavor

1. Browning and Caramelization:

- Browning vegetables, especially onions, carrots, and celery, develops a rich base for the stew. This step is similar to searing meat in traditional stews.

2. Umami Ingredients:

- Use umami-rich ingredients like mushrooms, soy sauce, tomato paste, nutritional yeast, or miso to mimic the savory depth of meat-based dishes.

3. Layered Cooking:

- Add ingredients in stages to create complexity. For example, add hearty vegetables like potatoes early and delicate greens like spinach toward the end.

4. Toasting Spices:

- Toast spices in oil to release their essential oils and deepen their flavor.

5. Using High-Quality Broth:

- A flavorful vegetable broth is essential. Homemade broths made with roasted vegetables and herbs provide the best base.

Pro Tip: Adding a splash of vinegar, lemon juice, or wine at the end of cooking brightens flavors and balances richness.

3. Ingredients That Add Complexity

Root Vegetables:

- Carrots, parsnips, and sweet potatoes provide natural sweetness and body.

Legumes:

- Lentils, chickpeas, and black beans add protein and a creamy texture.

Grains and Pasta:

- Barley, quinoa, rice, and small pasta shapes make stews heartier.

Dairy Alternatives:

- Coconut milk, cashew cream, and plant-based yogurts create creamy textures.

Herbs and Spices:

- Fresh herbs like thyme, parsley, and cilantro, along with spices like cumin, turmeric, and smoked paprika, bring depth and character.

Recipes: Vegetarian and Vegan Stews

1. Ratatouille

Ratatouille is a French vegetable stew that combines the flavors of zucchini, eggplant, peppers, and tomatoes in a simple yet elegant dish. It's naturally vegan and celebrates the essence of Mediterranean cooking.

Ingredients (Serves 4):

- 2 tablespoons olive oil
- 1 onion, diced
- 3 garlic cloves, minced
- 1 eggplant, diced
- 2 zucchini, diced

- 1 red bell pepper, diced
- 4 medium tomatoes, chopped (or 1 can diced tomatoes)
- 1 teaspoon thyme
- 1 teaspoon dried basil
- Salt and pepper to taste
- Fresh parsley for garnish

Instructions:

1. Sauté the Onion and Garlic: Heat olive oil in a pot. Sauté onion and garlic until softened.

2. Add Vegetables: Add eggplant, zucchini, and bell pepper. Cook until slightly softened.

3. Build the Stew: Stir in tomatoes, thyme, basil, salt, and pepper. Simmer for 20-25 minutes, stirring occasionally.

4. Serve: Garnish with fresh parsley and serve with crusty bread or over rice.

Pro Tip: For extra flavor, roast the vegetables before adding them to the pot.

2. Vegetable Curry Stew

This vibrant stew combines seasonal vegetables with aromatic spices and creamy coconut milk, making it a hearty vegan dish perfect for any occasion.

Ingredients (Serves 4):

- 2 tablespoons vegetable oil
- 1 onion, diced
- 2 garlic cloves, minced
- 1 tablespoon grated ginger
- 2 tablespoons curry powder
- 1 teaspoon turmeric
- 1 can (14 oz) coconut milk
- 2 cups vegetable broth
- 2 cups diced sweet potatoes
- 1 cup cauliflower florets
- 1 cup spinach leaves
- 1 cup cooked chickpeas
- Juice of 1 lime

- Fresh cilantro for garnish

Instructions:

1. Cook the Aromatics: Heat oil in a pot. Sauté onion, garlic, and ginger until fragrant. Stir in curry powder and turmeric.

2. Add Coconut Milk and Broth: Stir in coconut milk and vegetable broth. Bring to a simmer.

3. Cook Vegetables: Add sweet potatoes and cauliflower. Simmer for 15-20 minutes, or until vegetables are tender.

4. Finish the Stew: Stir in spinach and chickpeas. Cook for 2-3 minutes. Add lime juice and adjust seasoning.

5. Serve: Garnish with cilantro and serve with steamed rice or naan.

Pro Tip: For a spicier stew, add red chili flakes or a diced jalapeño.

3. Black Bean Chili

Black bean chili is a bold, satisfying dish that pairs the earthy flavor of beans with smoky spices. It's easy to make, protein-packed, and perfect for a crowd.

Ingredients (Serves 4):

- 2 tablespoons olive oil
- 1 onion, diced
- 3 garlic cloves, minced
- 1 red bell pepper, diced
- 1 tablespoon chili powder
- 1 teaspoon cumin
- 1 teaspoon smoked paprika
- 1 can (14 oz) diced tomatoes
- 2 cans (14 oz each) black beans, rinsed and drained
- 1 cup vegetable broth
- 1 cup corn kernels (fresh or frozen)
- Salt and pepper to taste
- Avocado, lime wedges, and fresh cilantro for garnish

Instructions:

1. Cook the Aromatics: Heat olive oil in a pot. Sauté onion, garlic, and bell pepper until softened.

2. Add Spices: Stir in chili powder, cumin, and smoked paprika. Cook for 1 minute.

3. Build the Chili: Add tomatoes, black beans, and vegetable broth. Simmer for 20 minutes.

4. Add Corn: Stir in corn and cook for 5 minutes. Adjust seasoning with salt and pepper.

5. Serve: Garnish with avocado, lime wedges, and cilantro.

Pro Tip: Add a square of dark chocolate to the chili for a subtle richness.

Using Plant-Based Proteins and Dairy Substitutes

1. Plant-Based Proteins

Legumes:

- Lentils, chickpeas, and black beans are rich in protein and fiber, making them ideal for stews.

Tofu and Tempeh:

- These soy-based proteins absorb flavors well and add a satisfying texture.

Grains and Seeds:

- Quinoa, farro, and bulgur provide a protein boost and a chewy texture.

2. Dairy Substitutes

Coconut Milk:

- Adds creaminess and a subtle sweetness, perfect for curries and stews.

Cashew Cream:

- Blended cashews create a rich, dairy-free cream alternative.

Plant-Based Yogurts:

- Use unsweetened almond or soy yogurt for tangy stews.

3. Enhancing Texture and Flavor

Mushrooms:

- Their umami flavor and meaty texture mimic the depth of meat-based stews.

Nutritional Yeast:

- Adds a cheesy, nutty flavor to vegan dishes.
Fermented Ingredients:
- Miso, kimchi, or sauerkraut add tanginess and depth.

Balancing Ingredients in Plant-Based Stews

1. Creating Harmony

Balance hearty ingredients (potatoes, beans) with light elements (greens, herbs) to avoid heaviness.

2. Brightening the Dish

Acidity from lime, lemon, or vinegar cuts through richness and enhances flavor.

Closing Thoughts

Vegetarian and vegan stews are a testament to the creativity and depth of plant-based cooking. By mastering these techniques and recipes, you'll be able to create dishes that satisfy every palate while celebrating the natural goodness of vegetables, legumes, and grains. In the next chapter, we'll explore rustic and hearty stews that highlight the beauty of simple, countryside cooking. Let's keep cooking!

Chapter 10: Rustic and Hearty Stews

Rustic and hearty stews embody the spirit of country cooking, offering warmth, sustenance, and simplicity in a single pot. These stews, often made with humble ingredients, are elevated by slow cooking techniques and the use of seasonal produce. They evoke the charm of farmhouse kitchens and the satisfaction of a meal shared around a communal table.

In this chapter, we'll explore the essence of rustic stews, share recipes for three classic dishes—lamb stew, pork and cider stew, and barley mushroom stew—and delve into the techniques for building deep, layered flavors using fresh, seasonal ingredients.

The Charm of Country-Style One-Pot Meals

1. What Defines Rustic Stews?

Rustic stews are characterized by their simplicity, heartiness, and reliance on local, seasonal ingredients. These dishes often reflect the ingenuity of rural communities, where cooks transformed available resources into nourishing meals.

Key Features of Rustic Stews:

- One-Pot Cooking: Everything is cooked together, allowing flavors to meld.

- Hearty Ingredients: Root vegetables, grains, and robust proteins make these stews filling.

- Slow Cooking: Time is the secret ingredient, allowing flavors to deepen and ingredients to tenderize.

Pro Tip: Rustic stews often taste better the next day, as the flavors continue to develop.

2. The Cultural Significance of Hearty Stews

In many cultures, hearty stews are more than just meals—they are symbols of tradition, hospitality, and resilience. Whether it's a lamb stew simmering in an Irish cottage or a mushroom barley stew warming a Hungarian farmhouse, these dishes tell stories of resourcefulness and community.

Examples:

- Irish Lamb Stew: A staple of Irish households, this dish showcases the country's agricultural heritage.

- French Cassoulet: A slow-cooked bean and meat stew that celebrates the bounty of the countryside.

- Eastern European Barley Stews: Highlighting the role of grains in sustaining rural communities.

Recipes: Rustic and Hearty Stews

1. Lamb Stew

Lamb stew is a classic comfort food, blending tender meat with root vegetables and a rich, savory broth. This dish is deeply rooted in Irish and Mediterranean traditions.

Ingredients (Serves 4):

- 2 pounds lamb shoulder, cut into chunks
- 2 tablespoons olive oil
- 1 onion, diced
- 3 garlic cloves, minced
- 3 carrots, sliced
- 2 celery stalks, sliced
- 4 medium potatoes, peeled and cubed
- 4 cups beef or lamb broth
- 1 cup red wine
- 2 tablespoons tomato paste
- 1 teaspoon thyme
- 1 bay leaf
- Salt and pepper to taste
- Fresh parsley for garnish

Instructions:

1. Brown the Lamb: Heat olive oil in a large pot. Sear lamb chunks until browned on all sides. Remove and set aside.

2. Sauté Vegetables: Add onion, garlic, carrots, and celery to the pot. Cook until softened.

3. Build the Broth: Stir in tomato paste, thyme, and bay leaf. Add wine, scraping up browned bits. Return lamb to the pot and add broth.

4. Simmer: Cover and simmer on low heat for 2 hours. Add potatoes in the last 30 minutes of cooking.

5. Season and Serve: Remove bay leaf, season with salt and pepper, and garnish with parsley. Serve with crusty bread.

Pro Tip: For added richness, stir in a tablespoon of Worcestershire sauce or balsamic vinegar before serving.

2. Pork and Cider Stew

This hearty stew combines the richness of pork with the sweetness of cider, creating a dish that is both comforting and slightly tangy.

Ingredients (Serves 4):

- 2 pounds pork shoulder, cut into chunks
- 2 tablespoons butter
- 1 onion, diced
- 3 garlic cloves, minced
- 2 cups hard apple cider
- 2 cups chicken broth
- 3 medium apples, peeled and sliced
- 3 carrots, sliced
- 2 parsnips, sliced
- 1 teaspoon sage
- 1 teaspoon thyme
- Salt and pepper to taste

Instructions:

1. Brown the Pork: Melt butter in a large pot. Sear pork chunks until browned. Remove and set aside.

2. Cook the Aromatics: Add onion and garlic to the pot. Cook until softened.

3. Build the Broth: Stir in cider, broth, sage, and thyme. Return pork to the pot.

4. Add Vegetables and Apples: Add carrots, parsnips, and apples. Cover and simmer for 1.5 to 2 hours, or until pork is tender.

5. Season and Serve: Adjust seasoning with salt and pepper. Serve with mashed potatoes or crusty bread.

Pro Tip: For a deeper flavor, use smoked paprika or a splash of brandy.

3. Barley Mushroom Stew

Barley mushroom stew is a vegetarian delight that highlights the earthy flavors of mushrooms and the nutty texture of barley. It's a wholesome, satisfying meal perfect for chilly evenings.

Ingredients (Serves 4):

- 2 tablespoons olive oil
- 1 onion, diced
- 3 garlic cloves, minced
- 1 pound mushrooms (button, cremini, or shiitake), sliced
- 1 cup pearl barley
- 6 cups vegetable broth
- 2 carrots, diced
- 2 celery stalks, diced
- 1 teaspoon thyme
- 1 bay leaf
- 1/2 cup dry white wine (optional)
- Salt and pepper to taste
- Fresh parsley for garnish

Instructions:

1. Cook the Aromatics: Heat olive oil in a pot. Sauté onion, garlic, carrots, and celery until softened.

2. Cook the Mushrooms: Add mushrooms and cook until browned.

3. Add Barley and Broth: Stir in barley, thyme, bay leaf, and vegetable broth. Bring to a simmer.

4. Simmer: Cover and cook for 40-50 minutes, or until barley is tender. Stir in white wine, if using.

5. Season and Serve: Remove bay leaf, season with salt and pepper, and garnish with parsley.

Pro Tip: Add a splash of soy sauce or miso for an umami boost.

How to Build Flavors with Seasonal Produce

1. The Role of Seasonal Ingredients

Seasonal produce not only enhances flavor but also reflects the natural rhythm of the land. By incorporating what's fresh and available, rustic stews become more vibrant and satisfying.

Seasonal Produce Examples:
- Fall: Pumpkins, squash, apples, and root vegetables.
- Winter: Potatoes, carrots, parsnips, and cabbage.
- Spring: Asparagus, peas, leeks, and baby greens.
- Summer: Tomatoes, zucchini, bell peppers, and corn.

Pro Tip: Pair seasonal vegetables with complementary herbs and spices to create a cohesive flavor profile.

2. Techniques for Maximizing Flavor

1. Roasting Vegetables:
- Roasting root vegetables before adding them to the stew caramelizes their natural sugars and deepens their flavor.

2. Using Fresh Herbs:
- Add hardy herbs like thyme and rosemary early in cooking and delicate herbs like parsley and dill at the end.

3. Balancing Sweetness and Acidity:
- Use ingredients like cider, vinegar, or tomatoes to balance the natural sweetness of vegetables.

4. Thickening with Starches:
- Potatoes, barley, and lentils naturally thicken the stew, adding both body and texture.

3. Pairing Ingredients for Harmony

Rustic stews often shine when ingredients are paired thoughtfully:

- Lamb and Root Vegetables: Earthy vegetables complement the richness of lamb.

- Pork and Apples: The sweetness of apples balances the savory depth of pork.

- Mushrooms and Barley: Both ingredients share an earthy, nutty profile, creating a harmonious dish.

Serving Rustic Stews

1. Side Dishes:
    - Bread: Crusty sourdough or buttery biscuits.
    - Salads: A simple green salad with vinaigrette.
    - Grains: Steamed rice or creamy polenta.
2. Garnishes:
- Fresh herbs, a drizzle of olive oil, or a dollop of sour cream enhance both flavor and presentation.

Closing Thoughts

Rustic and hearty stews celebrate the beauty of simplicity, turning basic ingredients into extraordinary meals. By mastering the recipes and techniques in this chapter, you'll be able to create dishes that warm the heart and soul, bringing the charm of countryside cooking into your home. In the next chapter, we'll explore light and healthy stews, perfect for those seeking nourishment with a lighter touch. Let's continue cooking!

Chapter 11: Stock and Broth Essentials

Stocks and broths are the foundational building blocks of soups and stews, providing depth, flavor, and body. A well-made stock or broth can elevate a dish from ordinary to extraordinary, adding layers of complexity and richness that are impossible to achieve with store-bought alternatives. By mastering the art of making homemade stocks, you'll unlock the key to creating soups and stews that truly shine.

This chapter explores the essentials of stock and broth, provides detailed recipes for chicken, beef, vegetable, and seafood stocks, explains how to store and freeze stock for future use, and highlights why homemade stocks are a game-changer for any soup or stew.

The Importance of Stocks and Broths

1. What Are Stocks and Broths?

Stocks and broths are both liquids made by simmering water with bones, vegetables, and aromatics, but they serve slightly different purposes in cooking.
Stocks:
- Made primarily with bones, which release collagen as they simmer, giving the liquid a gelatinous texture when cooled.
- Rich and flavorful, stocks are used as a base for soups, stews, and sauces.
Broths:
- Typically made with meat and fewer bones, resulting in a lighter, clearer liquid.
- Often seasoned and served as a standalone dish.
2. Why Homemade Stocks Are Superior
While store-bought stocks and broths are convenient, they often lack the depth and nuance of homemade versions.
Advantages of Homemade Stocks:
- Control Over Ingredients: You decide the seasoning, salt content, and flavor profile.

- Depth of Flavor: Simmering bones and vegetables for hours creates a richer, more complex taste.

- Health Benefits: Homemade stocks are free from preservatives and often contain nutrients like calcium and gelatin from the bones.

- Customizable: Tailor your stock to suit the recipe by adjusting ingredients and aromatics.

Pro Tip: Use leftover scraps from vegetables and bones to make stocks, reducing waste while enhancing flavor.

Recipes for Homemade Stocks

1. Chicken Stock

Chicken stock is versatile and perfect for soups, stews, and sauces. Its mild flavor pairs well with a wide variety of dishes.

Ingredients:

- 2 pounds chicken bones (carcass, wings, or necks)
- 1 onion, quartered
- 2 carrots, chopped
- 2 celery stalks, chopped
- 3 garlic cloves, smashed
- 1 bay leaf
- 1 teaspoon black peppercorns
- 10 cups water

Instructions:

1. Prepare the Ingredients: Rinse chicken bones to remove impurities.

2. Simmer: Place all ingredients in a large pot and cover with water. Bring to a boil, then reduce heat to a gentle simmer.

3. Skim Impurities: Skim off foam and fat that rise to the surface during the first 30 minutes.

4. Cook: Simmer uncovered for 3-4 hours.

5. Strain: Strain the stock through a fine-mesh sieve. Cool and store.

Pro Tip: For a richer stock, roast the chicken bones before simmering.

2. Beef Stock

Beef stock has a robust flavor, ideal for hearty soups, stews, and gravies.

Ingredients:

- 3 pounds beef bones (marrow bones, shanks, or oxtails)
- 1 onion, quartered
- 2 carrots, chopped
- 2 celery stalks, chopped
- 2 garlic cloves, smashed
- 2 tablespoons tomato paste
- 1 bay leaf
- 1 teaspoon black peppercorns
- 12 cups water

Instructions:

1. Roast the Bones: Preheat the oven to 400°F. Place beef bones on a baking sheet and roast for 30-40 minutes, turning occasionally.

2. Combine Ingredients: Transfer roasted bones to a large pot. Add vegetables, tomato paste, and seasonings. Cover with water.

3. Simmer: Bring to a boil, reduce to a gentle simmer, and skim off impurities.

4. Cook: Simmer uncovered for 6-8 hours.

5. Strain: Strain through a fine-mesh sieve, cool, and store.

Pro Tip: Add a splash of vinegar to the pot to help extract minerals from the bones.

3. Vegetable Stock

Vegetable stock is light and flavorful, perfect for vegetarian and vegan dishes.

Ingredients:

- 1 onion, quartered
- 2 carrots, chopped
- 2 celery stalks, chopped
- 2 garlic cloves, smashed
- 1 cup mushrooms, sliced
- 1 bay leaf
- 1 teaspoon black peppercorns

- A handful of fresh parsley
- 8 cups water

Instructions:

1. Prepare Vegetables: Use fresh or leftover vegetable scraps. Avoid starchy or bitter vegetables like potatoes or broccoli.

2. Simmer: Combine all ingredients in a large pot. Cover with water and bring to a boil. Reduce heat and simmer for 45-60 minutes.

3. Strain: Strain the stock through a fine-mesh sieve. Cool and store.

Pro Tip: For a richer flavor, roast the vegetables before simmering.

4. Seafood Stock

Seafood stock is ideal for chowders, bisques, and paellas, offering a briny, oceanic flavor.

Ingredients:

- Shells from 1 pound shrimp or lobster
- 1 onion, diced
- 2 celery stalks, chopped
- 2 garlic cloves, smashed
- 1 bay leaf
- 1 teaspoon black peppercorns
- A few sprigs of thyme
- 8 cups water

Instructions:

1. Sauté Shells: Heat a large pot over medium heat. Sauté shrimp or lobster shells in a bit of oil until aromatic.

2. Add Vegetables and Aromatics: Stir in onion, celery, garlic, bay leaf, peppercorns, and thyme.

3. Simmer: Add water and bring to a boil. Reduce heat and simmer for 30-45 minutes.

4. Strain: Strain through a fine-mesh sieve. Cool and store.

Pro Tip: Add a splash of white wine for extra depth.

Storing and Freezing Stock for Future Use

1. Proper Storage Techniques

Homemade stocks are perishable and should be stored carefully to maintain their quality:

- Refrigeration: Store in airtight containers for up to 5 days.

- Freezing: Divide stock into smaller portions for easy use. Freeze in freezer-safe containers, zip-top bags, or ice cube trays.

Pro Tip: Label containers with the date and type of stock to avoid confusion.

2. Freezing Tips

Ice Cube Trays:

- Freeze stock in ice cube trays for small portions. Once frozen, transfer cubes to a zip-top bag.

Silicone Molds:

- Use silicone molds for slightly larger portions.

Avoid Overfilling:

- Liquids expand when frozen, so leave some headspace in containers.

3. Defrosting Stock

Refrigerator Method:

- Place frozen stock in the refrigerator overnight to thaw slowly.

Quick Method:

- Run the container under warm water to release the frozen stock, then heat it in a pot on the stove.

How Homemade Stocks Elevate Soups and Stews

1. Enhanced Flavor

Homemade stocks are richer and more nuanced than store-bought versions, adding depth and character to soups and stews.

2. Texture and Body

The natural gelatin in homemade stocks gives soups and stews a silky texture that enhances their mouthfeel.

3. Health Benefits

Homemade stocks are free from preservatives and often contain beneficial nutrients like collagen, calcium, and amino acids.

Using Stocks in Recipes

Chicken Stock:
- Ideal for chicken noodle soup, risottos, and light stews.

Beef Stock:
- Perfect for hearty beef stews, French onion soup, and gravies.

Vegetable Stock:
- Use in minestrone, vegetarian stews, and as a base for cooking grains.

Seafood Stock:
- Essential for chowders, bouillabaisse, and seafood risottos.

Closing Thoughts

Mastering the art of homemade stocks is a game-changer for anyone passionate about cooking. With these recipes, storage tips, and insights, you'll be able to create soups and stews that truly stand out. In the next chapter, we'll explore thickening techniques, diving into the methods that give soups and stews their signature textures. Let's continue perfecting the craft!

Chapter 12: Thickening Techniques

Thickening soups and stews is an art that transforms simple liquids into luscious, hearty dishes with satisfying textures. Whether it's a velvety bisque, a robust stew, or a creamy chowder, the right thickening technique can elevate the eating experience and enhance the flavors of your dish. From classic roux to modern gluten-free alternatives, there are numerous ways to achieve the perfect consistency.

This chapter explores the science and application of various thickening techniques, including roux, slurry, and other agents. It also provides a detailed guide to achieving the ideal texture while catering to dietary needs with gluten-free and dairy-free options.

Understanding Thickening Agents

1. The Role of Thickening Agents

Thickening agents are used to:
- Enhance Texture: Creating a creamy or hearty mouthfeel.
- Improve Stability: Preventing ingredients from separating in the liquid.
- Bind Flavors: Encouraging flavors to coat ingredients evenly.

2. Common Types of Thickening Agents

1. Starch-Based Agents:
- These include flour, cornstarch, arrowroot, and tapioca.
- Work by absorbing liquid and swelling when heated.
2. Fat-Based Agents:
- Roux, butter, and cream thicken by adding richness and body.
3. Protein-Based Agents:
- Eggs and dairy proteins create a custard-like texture.
4. Natural Agents:
- Pureed vegetables, legumes, and grains provide body without added starches or fats.

Pro Tip: The choice of thickening agent depends on the dish's desired texture, flavor profile, and dietary considerations.

Classic Thickening Techniques

1. Roux

Roux is a classic French technique made by cooking equal parts flour and fat (typically butter). It serves as the foundation for many soups, stews, and sauces.

Types of Roux:

- White Roux: Cooked briefly, used in cream soups and béchamel sauce.

- Blond Roux: Cooked slightly longer for a nutty flavor, ideal for velouté and chowders.

- Brown Roux: Cooked until deep brown, used in hearty stews and gumbo.

How to Make a Roux:

1. Melt fat (butter, oil, or drippings) in a saucepan.

2. Stir in an equal amount of flour.

3. Cook over low heat, stirring constantly, until the desired color is achieved.

Pro Tip: Add the roux to your soup or stew gradually, whisking to prevent lumps.

2. Slurry

A slurry is a mixture of starch (cornstarch, arrowroot, or potato starch) and cold water or broth. It's added to hot liquids to thicken them quickly.

How to Make a Slurry:

1. Combine 1-2 tablespoons of starch with an equal amount of cold liquid.

2. Whisk until smooth.

3. Gradually stir into the simmering soup or stew.

Pro Tip: Avoid overcooking slurries made with cornstarch or arrowroot, as they can break down and lose their thickening power.

3. Beurre Manié

Beurre manié is a French technique similar to roux but is added raw. It's made by kneading equal parts butter and flour into a smooth paste, which is then whisked into hot liquids.

How to Use Beurre Manié:

1. Roll softened butter and flour into small balls.

2. Drop into the simmering liquid, whisking until dissolved.

Pro Tip: Beurre manié is ideal for last-minute thickening as it dissolves quickly without altering the flavor.

4. Reduction

Reducing a liquid by simmering or boiling evaporates water, concentrating flavors and thickening naturally.

How to Reduce:

1. Simmer uncovered, stirring occasionally, until the liquid volume decreases.

2. Use a wide pan for faster evaporation.

Pro Tip: Reduction works best for broths, wine-based sauces, and tomato-based stews.

Modern Thickening Techniques

1. Pureeing Ingredients

Pureeing part of the soup or stew adds natural thickness and body without additional ingredients.

How to Puree:

1. Use an immersion blender to blend ingredients directly in the pot.

2. For a smoother texture, transfer the mixture to a stand blender and blend in batches.

Best Ingredients for Pureeing:

- Potatoes, carrots, squash, beans, lentils, and tomatoes.

Pro Tip: For chunky stews, puree only a portion of the ingredients, leaving the rest intact for texture.

2. Dairy-Based Thickeners

1. Cream:
   - Adds richness and a silky texture, ideal for bisques and chowders.
   2. Yogurt:
   - Provides tanginess and a creamy consistency but should be added at the end to avoid curdling.
   3. Cheese:
   - Melts into the liquid for a thick, flavorful base (e.g., cheddar in broccoli cheese soup).
   Pro Tip: Use full-fat dairy to prevent curdling, and stir continuously when adding to hot liquids.

3. Egg Yolks

Egg yolks are a classic thickener for velvety soups like bisques and veloutés.
   How to Temper Egg Yolks:
   1. Beat yolks in a bowl.
   2. Gradually whisk in a small amount of hot liquid to raise the temperature without scrambling.
   3. Stir the tempered yolks back into the pot.
   Pro Tip: Avoid boiling after adding yolks to prevent curdling.

Gluten-Free and Dairy-Free Thickening Options

1. Gluten-Free Thickeners

1. Cornstarch:
   - Gluten-free and neutral in flavor.
   2. Arrowroot:
   - Works well for clear soups but can become slimy if overcooked.
   3. Tapioca Starch:
   - Adds a glossy finish, suitable for sweet and savory dishes.
   4. Rice Flour:
   - A versatile option for thickening and works similarly to all-purpose flour.

2. Dairy-Free Thickeners

1. Coconut Milk:
    - Adds creaminess with a subtle sweetness, perfect for curries and chowders.
2. Cashew Cream:
    - Blend soaked cashews with water for a rich, dairy-free alternative.
3. Plant-Based Yogurts:
    - Almond, soy, or oat yogurts provide tang and creaminess.
4. Nutritional Yeast:
    - Adds a cheesy, umami flavor to vegan soups and stews.

Achieving the Perfect Consistency

1. Key Tips for Perfectly Thickened Soups and Stews

- Start Gradually: Add thickeners in small amounts to avoid over-thickening.
    - Test the Texture: Use a spoon to check consistency before adding more thickener.
    - Stir Constantly: Prevent lumps and ensure even distribution.
    - Simmer, Don't Boil: Boiling can break down starch-based thickeners and curdle dairy.

2. Common Mistakes to Avoid

- Adding Starch Directly to Hot Liquid: Always mix starch with cold water first to avoid clumps.
    - Over-Thickening: Start with less thickener; you can always add more.
    - Neglecting to Stir: Inconsistent stirring can lead to uneven textures.

Recipes That Showcase Thickening Techniques

Creamy Potato Leek Soup (Roux)

Ingredients:
    - 2 tablespoons butter
    - 2 tablespoons flour
    - 4 leeks, sliced

- 4 cups chicken or vegetable broth
- 4 medium potatoes, diced
- 1 cup heavy cream
- Salt and pepper

Instructions:

1. Make a roux with butter and flour.
2. Add leeks and cook until softened.
3. Stir in broth and potatoes, simmer until tender.
4. Blend the soup and finish with cream.

Tomato Basil Soup (Slurry)

Ingredients:

- 1 tablespoon cornstarch
- 1 tablespoon cold water
- 4 cups diced tomatoes
- 1 onion, chopped
- 1 cup vegetable broth
- Fresh basil

Instructions:

1. Sauté onions and tomatoes.
2. Add broth and simmer.
3. Thicken with a cornstarch slurry and garnish with basil.

Vegan Mushroom Stew (Cashew Cream)

Ingredients:

- 1 cup cashews, soaked
- 2 cups mushrooms
- 1 onion, diced
- 4 cups vegetable broth

Instructions:

1. Blend soaked cashews into a cream.
2. Sauté mushrooms and onions.
3. Simmer with broth, then stir in cashew cream.

Closing Thoughts

Mastering thickening techniques is essential for creating soups and stews with rich, satisfying textures. By understanding and applying these methods, you'll have the tools to craft dishes tailored to your taste and dietary needs. In the next chapter, we'll explore garnishes and finishing touches, discovering how to elevate your creations with flair and flavor. Let's keep cooking!

Chapter 13: One-Pot Wonders

One-pot soups and stews are the epitome of comfort and convenience, combining simplicity with deep, robust flavors. These dishes minimize cleanup while maximizing taste, making them a favorite for busy cooks and food lovers alike. Whether it's a hearty chili con carne, the bold, spiced flavors of jambalaya, or the creamy comfort of split pea soup, one-pot wonders offer a diverse range of meals to suit every palate.

In this chapter, we'll explore the principles of creating flavorful one-pot dishes, provide detailed recipes for three iconic one-pot soups and stews, and discuss how to adapt these recipes for slow cookers and pressure cookers to make cooking even more convenient.

Maximizing Flavor and Convenience with One-Pot Soups and Stews

1. The Appeal of One-Pot Cooking

One-pot cooking simplifies the culinary process while delivering rich and complex flavors. By using a single pot, you can create meals that are as practical as they are delicious.

Advantages of One-Pot Cooking:

- Ease of Preparation: Everything is cooked in the same pot, reducing steps and time.

- Minimal Cleanup: Fewer dishes mean less time cleaning and more time enjoying your meal.

- Layered Flavors: Ingredients cook together, allowing flavors to meld and intensify.

- Versatility: Adaptable to a wide variety of cuisines and ingredients.

2. Building Flavor in a Single Pot

Creating depth of flavor in one-pot dishes requires thoughtful layering of ingredients and techniques.

Key Techniques:

1. Searing Proteins: Brown meat or seafood first to develop a caramelized crust and deepen the flavor of the base.

2. Sautéing Aromatics: Cook onions, garlic, and spices in the same pot to release their oils and build a flavorful foundation.

3. Deglazing: Use wine, broth, or water to scrape up browned bits from the bottom of the pot, adding complexity to the dish.

4. Simmering: Allowing ingredients to cook together over time enhances their flavors and creates a harmonious dish.

Pro Tip: Taste and adjust seasoning throughout the cooking process for the best results.

Recipes: Iconic One-Pot Soups and Stews

1. Chili con Carne

Chili con carne is a hearty, spiced stew featuring tender beef, beans, and tomatoes. This Tex-Mex classic is a crowd-pleaser, perfect for game days or cozy evenings.

Ingredients (Serves 4-6):

- 2 tablespoons olive oil
- 1 onion, diced
- 3 garlic cloves, minced
- 1 pound ground beef (or turkey for a lighter version)
- 1 red bell pepper, diced
- 2 tablespoons chili powder
- 1 teaspoon cumin
- 1 teaspoon smoked paprika
- 1 can (14 oz) diced tomatoes
- 1 can (14 oz) kidney beans, drained and rinsed

- 1 cup beef or chicken broth
- Salt and pepper to taste
- Optional toppings: sour cream, shredded cheese, chopped cilantro

Instructions:

1. Sauté Aromatics: Heat olive oil in a large pot. Sauté onion and garlic until softened.

2. Brown the Beef: Add ground beef and cook until browned. Drain excess fat if necessary.

3. Add Spices and Vegetables: Stir in bell pepper, chili powder, cumin, and smoked paprika. Cook for 1-2 minutes.

4. Build the Stew: Add tomatoes, beans, and broth. Simmer uncovered for 30-40 minutes, stirring occasionally.

5. Season and Serve: Adjust seasoning with salt and pepper. Serve with your favorite toppings.

Pro Tip: For a spicier chili, add diced jalapeños or a pinch of cayenne pepper.

2. Jambalaya

Jambalaya is a Creole and Cajun dish that combines rice, sausage, shrimp, and spices in a flavorful, hearty one-pot meal.

Ingredients (Serves 4-6):
- 2 tablespoons olive oil
- 1 pound andouille sausage, sliced
- 1 onion, diced
- 2 celery stalks, diced
- 1 green bell pepper, diced
- 3 garlic cloves, minced
- 2 cups long-grain rice
- 4 cups chicken broth
- 1 can (14 oz) diced tomatoes
- 1 tablespoon Cajun seasoning
- 1 teaspoon thyme
- 1 pound shrimp, peeled and deveined
- Salt and pepper to taste

- Fresh parsley for garnish
Instructions:

1. Cook the Sausage: Heat olive oil in a large pot. Brown the sausage slices, then remove and set aside.

2. Sauté Vegetables: Add onion, celery, bell pepper, and garlic. Cook until softened.

3. Add Rice and Spices: Stir in rice, Cajun seasoning, and thyme. Cook for 1-2 minutes to toast the rice.

4. Build the Dish: Add broth, tomatoes, and sausage. Bring to a boil, then reduce heat to a simmer. Cover and cook for 20-25 minutes, or until rice is tender.

5. Add Shrimp: Stir in shrimp and cook for 5-7 minutes, or until shrimp are pink and cooked through.

6. Season and Serve: Adjust seasoning with salt and pepper. Garnish with parsley before serving.

Pro Tip: For a smoky flavor, add a dash of smoked paprika or chipotle powder.

3. Split Pea Soup

Split pea soup is a comforting, protein-rich dish made with dried split peas, vegetables, and ham (or a plant-based alternative). It's a classic cold-weather meal.

Ingredients (Serves 4-6):
- 2 tablespoons butter or olive oil
- 1 onion, diced
- 2 carrots, diced
- 2 celery stalks, diced
- 2 garlic cloves, minced
- 2 cups dried split peas, rinsed and drained
- 6 cups chicken or vegetable broth
- 1 smoked ham hock or 1 cup diced smoked ham (optional)
- 1 bay leaf
- 1 teaspoon thyme
- Salt and pepper to taste

Instructions:

1. Sauté Aromatics: Heat butter or olive oil in a large pot. Sauté onion, carrots, celery, and garlic until softened.

2. Add Split Peas and Broth: Stir in split peas, broth, ham (if using), bay leaf, and thyme. Bring to a boil.

3. Simmer: Reduce heat to low, cover, and simmer for 1.5-2 hours, stirring occasionally. Remove bay leaf before serving.

4. Season and Serve: Adjust seasoning with salt and pepper. Serve with crusty bread.

Pro Tip: For a creamier texture, use an immersion blender to partially blend the soup.

Adapting Recipes for Slow Cookers and Pressure Cookers

1. Using a Slow Cooker

Slow cookers are perfect for one-pot dishes, allowing ingredients to simmer gently over several hours.

How to Adapt Recipes:

1. Brown Ingredients First: Sear meats and sauté aromatics on the stovetop before adding them to the slow cooker for added flavor.

2. Adjust Liquid Levels: Use slightly less liquid, as slow cookers don't allow for evaporation.

3. Cooking Times: Most recipes can be cooked on low for 6-8 hours or high for 3-4 hours.

Pro Tip: Add delicate ingredients, like shrimp or fresh herbs, in the last 30 minutes of cooking.

2. Using a Pressure Cooker (e.g., Instant Pot)

Pressure cookers speed up the cooking process, making them ideal for quick and flavorful meals.

How to Adapt Recipes:

1. Sauté First: Use the sauté function to brown ingredients before pressure cooking.

2. Reduce Cooking Times: Most stews cook in 15-30 minutes under high pressure.

3. Release Pressure: Allow for a natural pressure release for 10-15 minutes before opening the lid to maintain the dish's texture.

Pro Tip: Thickening agents like roux or slurry should be added after pressure cooking to avoid clumping.

Tips for One-Pot Success

1. Prep Ingredients Ahead: Have all ingredients measured and ready to streamline the process.

2. Layer Ingredients: Add longer-cooking ingredients (like root vegetables) first and delicate items (like seafood) later.

3. Monitor Liquid Levels: Check periodically to ensure the liquid hasn't evaporated too much, adding more broth if needed.

4. Season Gradually: Add salt and spices incrementally, tasting as you go.

Closing Thoughts

One-pot soups and stews combine the best of flavor and convenience, making them staples in kitchens worldwide. By mastering the techniques and recipes in this chapter, you'll have a repertoire of dishes that satisfy both your taste buds and your schedule. Whether you're cooking on the stovetop, in a slow cooker, or with a pressure cooker, these meals are sure to become family favorites. In the next chapter, we'll explore international soups and stews, diving into global flavors that bring the world to your table. Let's keep cooking!

Chapter 14: Garnishes and Sides

Soup and stew recipes may shine on their own, but it's often the garnishes and sides that elevate them from satisfying meals to unforgettable dining experiences. The right garnish can enhance a dish's flavor, add texture, and create visual appeal, while thoughtfully paired sides can round out the meal. Whether it's a swirl of herb oil, a sprinkling of fresh herbs, or a perfectly toasted crouton, garnishes and sides are the finishing touches that bring your soups and stews to life.

In this chapter, we'll explore the art of garnishing soups and stews, share recipes for versatile garnishes like croutons and herb oils, and provide tips on pairing soups and stews with breads, rice, and salads.

Elevating Soups and Stews with the Right Garnishes

1. The Purpose of Garnishes

Garnishes aren't just decorative—they serve important functions in enhancing the dining experience:

- Flavor: Add complementary or contrasting notes to the dish.
- Texture: Introduce crunch, creaminess, or freshness to balance the soup or stew's consistency.
- Visual Appeal: Create a polished, professional look.

Pro Tip: A garnish should always be edible and enhance the dish's overall flavor profile.

2. Types of Garnishes

1. Fresh Herbs:
   - Cilantro, parsley, thyme, dill, and chives add brightness and a burst of flavor.
   2. Dairy-Based Garnishes:
   - Swirls of sour cream, crème fraîche, or yogurt add creaminess and tang.
   - Shredded cheese (cheddar, Parmesan) melts beautifully into hot soups.
   3. Crunchy Toppings:

- Croutons, toasted seeds, or crispy fried onions provide texture and contrast.

4. Flavorful Oils:

- Herb oils, chili oil, or a drizzle of olive oil add depth and richness.

5. Acidic Accents:

- A squeeze of lemon or lime juice, a splash of vinegar, or pickled vegetables balance richness and brighten flavors.

6. Spice and Heat:

- A sprinkle of chili flakes, smoked paprika, or a dash of hot sauce adds heat and complexity.

Pro Tip: Balance garnishes so they don't overpower the main dish. For example, a hearty stew benefits from fresh herbs or a dollop of cream to lighten its richness.

Recipes for Garnishes

1. Croutons

Homemade croutons are an easy way to add crunch and flavor to soups and stews.

Ingredients:

- 4 slices of day-old bread, cut into cubes
- 2 tablespoons olive oil or melted butter
- 1 teaspoon garlic powder
- 1 teaspoon dried herbs (thyme, rosemary, or parsley)
- Salt and pepper to taste

Instructions:

1. Preheat the Oven: Heat oven to 375°F (190°C).

2. Prepare the Bread: Toss bread cubes with olive oil, garlic powder, herbs, salt, and pepper.

3. Bake: Spread the cubes on a baking sheet in a single layer. Bake for 10-15 minutes, turning occasionally, until golden and crisp.

4. Cool and Serve: Let cool before sprinkling on soups or stews.

Pro Tip: Add grated Parmesan cheese to the bread cubes before baking for extra flavor.

2. Herb Oil

A drizzle of herb oil adds freshness and visual appeal to soups.

Ingredients:

- 1/2 cup fresh herbs (basil, parsley, or cilantro)
- 1/4 cup olive oil
- 1 garlic clove (optional)
- Pinch of salt

Instructions:

1. Blend Ingredients: Combine herbs, olive oil, garlic (if using), and salt in a blender or food processor. Blend until smooth.

2. Strain (Optional): Strain through a fine-mesh sieve for a smooth finish.

3. Store and Use: Store in an airtight container in the refrigerator for up to a week.

Pro Tip: Use herb oil to add a pop of color and flavor to creamy soups like tomato bisque or potato leek soup.

3. Sour Cream Swirl

A sour cream swirl adds tanginess and a creamy texture to soups.

Ingredients:

- 1/4 cup sour cream
- 2 tablespoons milk or cream
- Pinch of salt

Instructions:

1. Whisk Together: In a small bowl, whisk sour cream, milk, and salt until smooth.

2. Swirl: Use a spoon to drizzle the mixture in a spiral or design on the surface of the soup.

Pro Tip: For a colorful variation, mix in a pinch of smoked paprika or a drop of hot sauce.

4. Fresh Herb Garnish

Fresh herbs are the simplest yet most effective garnish.

Instructions:

1. Wash and finely chop herbs like parsley, cilantro, or dill.

2. Sprinkle over the soup just before serving for a burst of freshness.

Pro Tip: Use whole herb sprigs for an elegant presentation.

Pairing Soups and Stews with Bread, Rice, and Salads

1. Bread: The Classic Companion

Bread is a timeless side that pairs beautifully with soups and stews, perfect for dipping or sopping up flavorful broths.

Types of Bread:

- Crusty Bread: Sourdough, baguette, or ciabatta is perfect for hearty stews.
- Flatbreads: Naan, pita, or focaccia pair well with spiced soups.
- Cornbread: A sweet and savory option for chili or Southern-style stews.
- Buttered Rolls: Ideal for creamy soups like clam chowder.

Pro Tip: Warm the bread in the oven before serving for a comforting touch.

2. Rice: A Hearty Base

Rice adds substance to soups and stews, making them more filling.

Types of Rice Pairings:

- Steamed White Rice: Pairs well with brothy soups like pho or miso soup.
- Brown Rice: Adds a nutty flavor to vegetable and lentil stews.
- Wild Rice: A chewy, earthy option for creamy chicken or mushroom soups.
- Rice Pilaf: Infused with herbs and spices, it complements Middle Eastern or Indian-inspired stews.

Pro Tip: Add cooked rice directly to the soup for a thicker, heartier dish.

3. Salads: Adding Freshness

Salads provide a refreshing contrast to the richness of soups and stews.

Simple Salad Pairings:

- Green Salad: Mixed greens with a light vinaigrette complement rich stews.

- Caesar Salad: A classic choice for pairing with creamy soups like potato leek.

- Coleslaw: A crunchy side for spicy stews like jambalaya.

- Cucumber Salad: Refreshing and cooling, ideal with spiced or curry-based stews.

Pro Tip: Incorporate ingredients from the soup or stew into the salad (e.g., fresh herbs or toasted nuts) for a cohesive meal.

Tips for Pairing Garnishes and Sides

1. Match Flavors: Choose garnishes and sides that complement the flavors of the dish. For example, pair herb oil with vegetable soups or cornbread with chili.

2. Balance Textures: Add crunchy elements to creamy soups or creamy garnishes to brothy soups.

3. Consider Temperature: Pair hot soups with cool sides like salads for contrast.

4. Keep It Simple: Let the soup or stew shine by choosing understated garnishes and sides.

Examples of Perfect Pairings

- Tomato Soup: Herb croutons and grilled cheese sandwiches.

- Beef Stew: Crusty bread and a simple green salad.

- Chicken Noodle Soup: Buttered rolls and a light cucumber salad.

- Lentil Soup: Flatbread and a tangy yogurt drizzle.

Closing Thoughts

Garnishes and sides are the final touches that transform soups and stews into memorable meals. By mastering these techniques and recipes, you'll be able to elevate your dishes with flair and flavor, creating meals that delight both the eyes and the palate. In the next chapter, we'll dive into international soups and stews, exploring global flavors and techniques to expand your culinary repertoire. Let's keep cooking!

Chapter 15: Cooking for Every Season

Cooking for every season means embracing the ingredients that shine during different times of the year. Soups and stews offer a versatile canvas to highlight seasonal produce, from hearty root vegetables in winter to light greens in spring, vibrant tomatoes in summer, and earthy mushrooms in fall. Adapting recipes to reflect seasonal availability not only enhances flavor but also aligns with sustainable and cost-effective cooking practices.

This chapter explores how to adapt soups and stews to seasonal ingredients, diving into specific recipes and techniques for winter, spring, summer, and fall. By understanding the unique flavors and characteristics of each season, you can create dishes that celebrate the natural bounty of the year.

Why Cook Seasonally?

1. Benefits of Seasonal Cooking

1. Enhanced Flavor:
    - Seasonal produce is harvested at peak ripeness, ensuring maximum flavor and freshness.
    2. Nutritional Value:
    - Produce grown and consumed in its natural season retains more nutrients.
    3. Sustainability:
    - Seasonal cooking reduces the carbon footprint associated with transporting out-of-season ingredients.
    4. Cost-Effectiveness:
    - Seasonal ingredients are often more affordable due to their abundance.
    Pro Tip: Visit local farmers' markets to explore what's fresh and in season.

2. Adapting Recipes to the Seasons

Each season brings its own set of ingredients and cooking techniques. Adjust recipes to highlight what's available:
    - Winter: Focus on slow-cooking techniques to draw out the flavors of root vegetables and meats.

- Spring: Emphasize fresh, delicate greens and herbs in lighter broths.

- Summer: Use minimal cooking for vibrant, chilled soups that showcase fresh produce.

- Fall: Incorporate earthy ingredients like squash, mushrooms, and grains in robust stews.

Winter: Hearty Stews with Root Vegetables

1. The Essence of Winter Cooking

Winter soups and stews are all about warmth and sustenance. Root vegetables like potatoes, carrots, parsnips, and turnips shine in these dishes, providing natural sweetness and a hearty texture.

Key Ingredients:

- Vegetables: Carrots, parsnips, sweet potatoes, rutabaga, and leeks.

- Proteins: Beef, lamb, chicken, or plant-based options like lentils and beans.

- Spices: Warm spices like cinnamon, nutmeg, and smoked paprika.

2. Recipe: Beef and Barley Stew

This classic winter stew combines tender beef with hearty barley and root vegetables.

Ingredients (Serves 6):

- 2 pounds beef chuck, cubed

- 2 tablespoons olive oil

- 1 onion, diced

- 2 carrots, sliced

- 2 celery stalks, sliced

- 3 garlic cloves, minced

- 1/2 cup pearl barley

- 6 cups beef broth

- 1 bay leaf

- 1 teaspoon thyme

- Salt and pepper to taste

Instructions:

1. Brown the Beef: Heat olive oil in a pot. Brown beef cubes and set aside.

2. Sauté Vegetables: Add onion, carrots, celery, and garlic. Cook until softened.

3. Build the Stew: Add barley, broth, bay leaf, and thyme. Return beef to the pot.

4. Simmer: Cover and simmer for 2-3 hours until beef is tender and barley is cooked.

5. Serve: Season with salt and pepper, and serve with crusty bread.

Pro Tip: Add a splash of red wine for extra depth.

Spring: Light Broths with Fresh Greens

1. The Essence of Spring Cooking

Spring soups celebrate renewal and freshness, using delicate greens, tender herbs, and young vegetables. The cooking methods are lighter, often involving quick simmering or steaming.

Key Ingredients:

- Vegetables: Asparagus, peas, leeks, spinach, and artichokes.

- Herbs: Mint, parsley, dill, and chives.

- Broths: Light vegetable or chicken broths.

2. Recipe: Spring Pea and Mint Soup

This vibrant soup captures the essence of spring with its bright flavors and light texture.

Ingredients (Serves 4):

- 2 tablespoons olive oil

- 1 onion, diced

- 3 cups fresh or frozen peas

- 4 cups vegetable broth

- 1/4 cup fresh mint leaves

- 1/2 cup heavy cream (optional)

- Salt and pepper to taste

Instructions:

1. Sauté Onion: Heat olive oil in a pot. Sauté onion until translucent.

2. Add Peas and Broth: Stir in peas and broth. Simmer for 10 minutes.

3. Blend: Puree the soup with mint leaves using an immersion blender.

4. Finish: Stir in cream (if using) and adjust seasoning. Serve with a dollop of yogurt or croutons.

Pro Tip: Garnish with a drizzle of herb oil for added freshness.

Summer: Chilled Soups with Vibrant Produce

1. The Essence of Summer Cooking

Summer soups are refreshing and highlight the abundance of ripe, juicy produce. Minimal cooking preserves the natural flavors and nutrients.

Key Ingredients:

- Vegetables: Tomatoes, cucumbers, bell peppers, and zucchini.

- Fruits: Watermelon, cantaloupe, and berries.

- Herbs: Basil, cilantro, and mint.

2. Recipe: Classic Gazpacho

Gazpacho is a chilled Spanish soup made with raw vegetables and a vibrant tomato base.

Ingredients (Serves 4):

- 4 ripe tomatoes, chopped

- 1 cucumber, peeled and diced

- 1 red bell pepper, chopped

- 2 garlic cloves

- 1/4 cup olive oil

- 2 tablespoons red wine vinegar

- 1 cup tomato juice

- Salt and pepper to taste

Instructions:

1. Blend Ingredients: Combine tomatoes, cucumber, bell pepper, garlic, olive oil, vinegar, and tomato juice in a blender. Blend until smooth.

2. Chill: Refrigerate for at least 2 hours.

3. Serve: Garnish with croutons or diced vegetables.

Pro Tip: Add a slice of stale bread to the blender for a thicker consistency.

Fall: Earthy Stews with Squash and Mushrooms

1. The Essence of Fall Cooking

Fall stews are rich, earthy, and comforting, often featuring ingredients like squash, mushrooms, and hearty grains. These dishes are perfect for cool evenings.

Key Ingredients:

- Vegetables: Butternut squash, pumpkin, and mushrooms.
- Grains: Farro, wild rice, and quinoa.
- Herbs: Sage, rosemary, and thyme.

2. Recipe: Butternut Squash and Mushroom Stew

This autumn-inspired stew pairs sweet squash with earthy mushrooms for a deeply satisfying dish.

Ingredients (Serves 4):

- 2 tablespoons olive oil
- 1 onion, diced
- 2 cups butternut squash, cubed
- 1 cup mushrooms, sliced
- 4 cups vegetable broth
- 1/2 cup farro
- 1 teaspoon sage
- Salt and pepper to taste

Instructions:

1. Sauté Vegetables: Heat olive oil in a pot. Sauté onion, squash, and mushrooms until softened.

2. Add Broth and Farro: Stir in broth, farro, and sage. Simmer for 30-40 minutes.

3. Season and Serve: Adjust seasoning with salt and pepper. Serve with crusty bread.

Pro Tip: Garnish with toasted pumpkin seeds for crunch.

Tips for Seasonal Cooking

1. Plan Ahead: Keep a list of seasonal ingredients and plan meals around their availability.

2. Visit Farmers' Markets: Explore fresh, local produce to inspire your recipes.

3. Store Smart: Freeze seasonal ingredients like berries or squash to enjoy later.

4. Experiment: Don't hesitate to substitute ingredients based on what's fresh and available.

Closing Thoughts

Cooking soups and stews for every season allows you to celebrate the best of what nature offers year-round. By adapting your recipes to seasonal ingredients, you'll create dishes that are fresher, more flavorful, and perfectly suited to the time of year. This journey through winter's hearty stews, spring's light broths, summer's refreshing soups, and fall's earthy creations concludes our exploration of seasonal cooking. Let the seasons guide your creativity in the kitchen, and continue crafting soups and stews that delight and nourish. Let's keep cooking!

Bonus Content: Enhancing Your Soup and Stew Game

Soup and stew lovers understand the appeal of these dishes beyond their delicious flavors. They're versatile, easy to prepare in batches, and perfect for meal prepping. This bonus chapter delves into practical tips for meal prepping soups and stews, freezing and reheating techniques, and a comprehensive glossary of essential herbs, spices, and ingredients to elevate your cooking.

Tips for Meal Prepping Soups and Stews

1. Why Meal Prep Soups and Stews?

Meal prepping soups and stews is a time-efficient way to enjoy homemade meals throughout the week. These dishes often taste better after resting, as flavors have more time to meld.

Benefits of Meal Prepping:

- Time-Saving: Prep once and enjoy multiple meals with minimal effort.
- Budget-Friendly: Use affordable ingredients and reduce food waste.
- Healthier Choices: Control ingredients, seasoning, and portion sizes.
- Convenience: Quickly reheat for a nutritious meal in minutes.

2. Planning for Success

Proper planning ensures meal prep is efficient and effective.

Steps to Plan Your Prep:

1. Choose Versatile Recipes: Select soups and stews that store and reheat well. Examples include chili, lentil soup, and chicken noodle soup.

2. Batch Cook: Prepare large quantities to maximize efficiency.

3. Invest in Storage Containers: Use airtight, freezer-safe containers in various sizes for flexibility.

4. Label Everything: Include the dish name and date to keep track of storage.

Pro Tip: Avoid adding delicate ingredients (like fresh herbs or cream) until just before serving to maintain freshness.

3. Portioning for Meal Prep

Portioning soups and stews correctly makes reheating easier and minimizes waste.

Portioning Tips:

- Single Servings: Use individual containers for grab-and-go convenience.

- Family-Sized Portions: Store larger quantities for family meals.

- Freezing in Layers: If freezing with toppings like noodles or rice, layer them separately to prevent sogginess.

Pro Tip: Freeze some portions in ice cube trays for easy use in smaller recipes or as quick flavor boosts for other dishes.

Freezing and Reheating Techniques for Batch Cooking

1. Freezing Soups and Stews

Proper freezing methods preserve the flavor and texture of your soups and stews.

Best Practices for Freezing:

1. Cool Completely: Allow soups to cool before freezing to prevent ice crystals and preserve texture.

2. Use Proper Containers: Choose freezer-safe bags, containers, or vacuum-sealed bags to prevent freezer burn.

3. Leave Room for Expansion: Liquids expand when frozen, so leave space at the top of containers.

What Freezes Well:

- Broth-based soups, chili, vegetable stews, and pureed soups like butternut squash.

What to Avoid Freezing:

- Cream-based soups (cream can separate) and soups with pasta (it can become mushy).

Pro Tip: Freeze soups flat in zip-top bags to save space and speed up thawing.

2. Reheating Soups and Stews

Reheating soups and stews correctly ensures they retain their original flavor and texture.

Reheating Tips:

- Stovetop: Place frozen soup in a pot over low heat. Add a splash of broth if needed. Stir occasionally to heat evenly.

- Microwave: Use a microwave-safe container, cover loosely, and reheat in 2-minute intervals, stirring between intervals.

- Slow Cooker: Reheat large batches directly in the slow cooker on low for 2-3 hours.

Pro Tip: Reheat cream-based soups gently over low heat, stirring constantly, to prevent curdling.

Glossary of Essential Herbs, Spices, and Ingredients

1. Essential Herbs

Herbs are the soul of soups and stews, adding freshness, aroma, and complexity.

Fresh Herbs:

- Parsley: Bright and grassy, ideal for garnishing and balancing flavors.

- Cilantro: Adds a citrusy, fresh flavor, especially in Mexican and Asian dishes.

- Thyme: Earthy and subtle, perfect for broths and hearty stews.

- Basil: Sweet and fragrant, pairs well with tomatoes and creamy soups.

- Dill: Fresh and slightly tangy, great for light broths and seafood stews.

Dried Herbs:

- Bay Leaves: Add depth to long-simmered soups and stews.

- Oregano: Strong and peppery, complements Mediterranean and Mexican dishes.

- Rosemary: Woody and aromatic, pairs well with lamb, chicken, and potatoes.

Pro Tip: Use dried herbs during cooking and fresh herbs as a garnish for the best balance of flavor.

2. Essential Spices

Spices add warmth, heat, and depth to soups and stews.

- Black Pepper: A universal seasoning that enhances overall flavor.
- Cumin: Earthy and slightly smoky, ideal for chili and Middle Eastern dishes.
- Paprika: Sweet or smoked, adds color and depth.
- Turmeric: Bright and earthy, a key ingredient in curries and lentil stews.
- Cinnamon: Warm and sweet, often used in Moroccan stews.
- Chili Powder: Adds heat and bold flavor, perfect for Tex-Mex dishes.

Pro Tip: Toast spices in a dry pan before adding them to your dish to release their essential oils.

3. Essential Ingredients

Broths and Stocks:

- The foundation of any soup or stew. Homemade stocks (chicken, beef, vegetable) provide superior flavor.

Proteins:

- Meat: Chicken thighs, beef chuck, lamb shanks, and pork shoulder are stew favorites.
- Legumes: Lentils, chickpeas, and black beans are excellent plant-based options.
- Seafood: Shrimp, clams, and fish work well in lighter stews.

Vegetables:

- Root Vegetables: Potatoes, carrots, and parsnips add heartiness.
- Greens: Spinach, kale, and chard add freshness and nutrition.
- Alliums: Onions, garlic, and leeks build a flavorful base.

Grains and Starches:

- Rice: Jasmine, basmati, and wild rice pair well with brothy soups.
- Pasta: Small shapes like orzo and ditalini are ideal for minestrone.
- Potatoes: Waxy potatoes hold their shape, while starchy ones thicken stews.

Bonus Tips for Perfect Soups and Stews

1. Balance Flavors: Use a combination of salty, sweet, sour, and umami elements to create depth.

2. Cook in Layers: Sauté aromatics, sear proteins, and simmer vegetables to build complexity.

3. Finish with Acidity: A splash of vinegar, citrus juice, or wine brightens flavors.

4. Adjust Consistency: Use thickeners like roux, pureed vegetables, or cream to reach the desired texture.

5. Taste and Adjust: Always taste as you go, adjusting seasoning to suit your palate.

Closing Thoughts

Meal prepping soups and stews, mastering freezing and reheating techniques, and understanding essential herbs, spices, and ingredients are invaluable tools for any home cook. These practices not only save time and effort but also ensure that every dish is flavorful, nourishing, and perfectly suited to your needs. Use this bonus content as a reference to enhance your cooking, and continue crafting soups and stews that delight and satisfy. Let's keep cooking!

Don't miss out!

Visit the website below and you can sign up to receive emails whenever Olivia Bennett publishes a new book. There's no charge and no obligation.

https://books2read.com/r/B-A-QLEKD-QNDAG

BOOKS 2 READ

Connecting independent readers to independent writers.

About the Author

Olivia Bennett is a celebrated food writer and chef with expertise spanning multiple culinary disciplines. With a passion for making home cooking accessible, she specializes in guiding readers through everything from hearty casseroles to delicate pastries. Her work is known for its clear instructions, practical tips, and deep understanding of both traditional and modern cooking techniques.